WITHDRAWN
From Toronto Public Library

DISCOVER CANADA

Yukon

By Anne Tempelman-Kluit

Consultants:

Desmond Morton, FRSC, Professor of History, University of Toronto

Trevor Bremner, M.Sc., P. Geol., Indian and Northern Affairs Canada, Yukon Region

Amanda Graham, Managing Editor, *Northern Review,* and Lecturer, Yukon College

Grolier Limited
TORONTO

Abandoned mine at Windy Arm, Tagish Lake, in the southern Yukon
Overleaf: Shakwak Valley, Kluane National Park

Dedication: For Dirk, who was there first

Canadian Cataloguing in Publication Data

Tempelman-Kluit, Anne, 1941-
  Yukon

(Discover Canada)
Rev. ed.
Includes index.
ISBN 0-7172-3149-6

1. Yukon Territory — Juvenile literature. I. Title. II. Series: Discover Canada (Toronto, Ont.).

FC4011.2.T45 1996   j971.9'1   C96-931901-0
F1091.4.T45 1996

Front cover: Fall in the Selwyn Mountains along the Yukon-Northwest Territories border
Back cover: Aerial view of St. Elias Mountains, Kluane National Park

Copyright © 1994, 1996 by Anne Tempelman-Kluit (text) and Grolier Ltd. All rights reserved. No part of this book may be reproduced or transmitted in any form or by any means, electronic or mechanical, including photocopying, or by any information storage and retrieval system, without permission in writing from the publisher.

Printed and bound in Canada.
Published simultaneously in the United States.
2 3 4 5 6 7 8 9 10   DWF   99 98 97 96

Signpost near Keno City

Table of Contents

Chapter 1　　Land of the Midnight Sun.....7
Chapter 2　　The Land.....9
Chapter 3　　First Peoples.....25
Chapter 4　　Fur Traders and Gold-Seekers.....35
Chapter 5　　New Transportation and a New North.....51
Chapter 6　　A New Territory and a Developing Government.....63
Chapter 7　　An Economic Portrait.....74
Chapter 8　　Arts and Recreation.....85
Chapter 9　　Touring the Territory.....95
Facts At a Glance.....109
Maps.....122
Index.....125

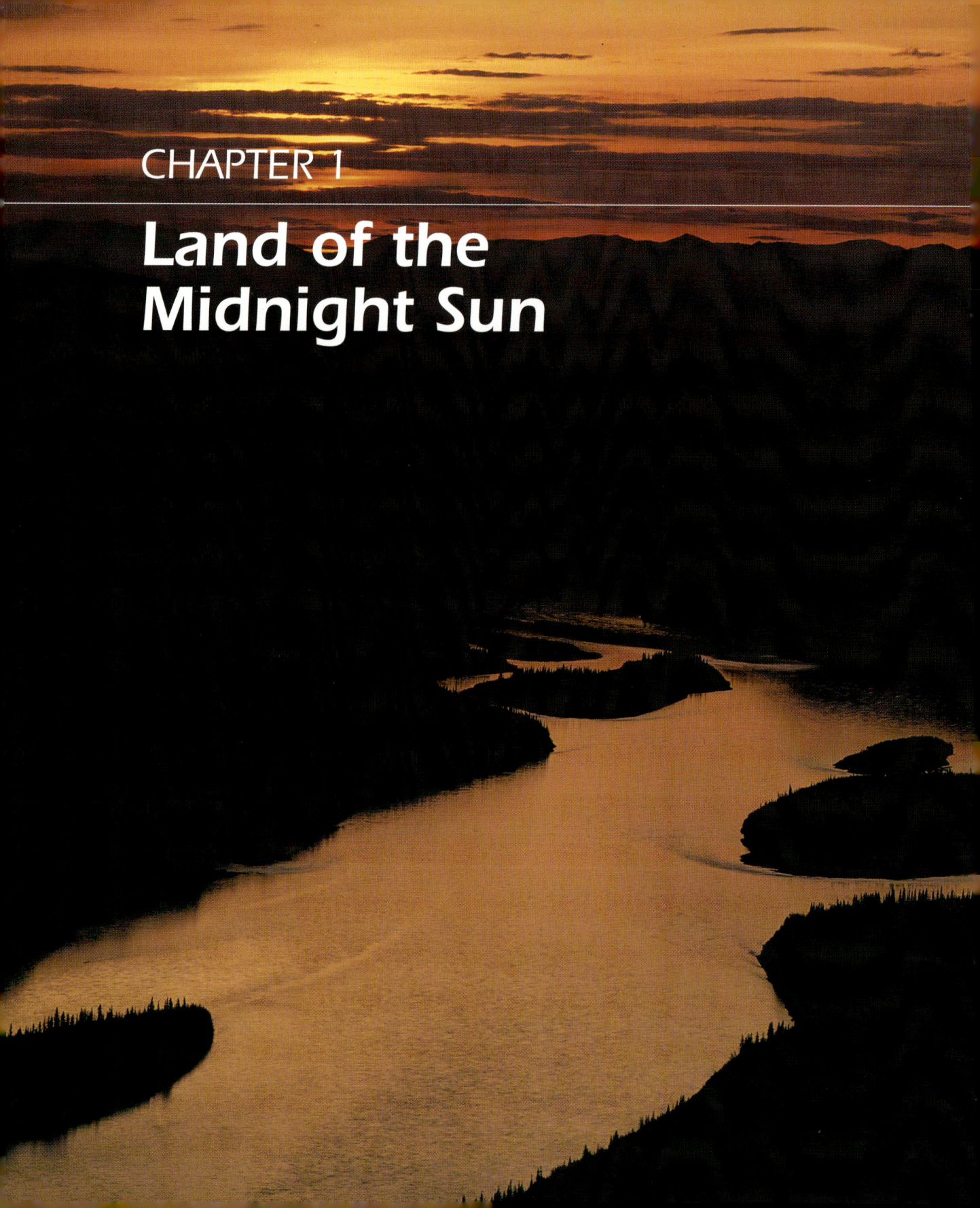

CHAPTER 1
Land of the Midnight Sun

The Yukon is both a Land of the Midnight Sun and a cold, dark land covered in snow, depending on the season of the year. Such contrasts are part of the grip this little-known territory holds for people "outside," as Yukoners call the rest of the world. The Yukon is a land of skyscraping mountain peaks, sprawling Arctic tundra, silent valleys and cold, pure lakes and rivers. Equally important to many today, it is also a land marked by human life, with highways, mines, power lines, city streets, art galleries, golf courses, restaurants, computer shops ....

A little over a hundred years ago, the Yukon River gave the territory its English-language name. The name came from the Gwich'in people's word for this "great river." For them and other Native peoples, the river had been an important transportation route for thousands of years.

In the 1800s the Yukon River became a highway to adventure for European fur traders, mappers and missionaries. After major deposits of gold were discovered near Dawson in 1896, it became a highway for thousands of gold-seekers who stormed into the Yukon to stake their claims in the Klondike goldfields.

Almost 50 years later, in 1942, a new wave of thousands of workers arrived to build the Alaska Highway, the modern equivalent of the famous river.

Today the diverse Yukon still attracts people with its rich mineral deposits and vivid history; its space and solitude; its challenge, opportunity and hope.

Welcome to the Land of the Midnight Sun.

CHAPTER 2
The Land

The Yukon Territory, located in the extreme northwestern part of Canada, is a triangular-shaped area of 483 450 square kilometres (186 700 square miles). The southernmost part of the triangle borders on the province of British Columbia. To the east are the Northwest Territories (NWT) and to the west, the American state of Alaska. At its northern boundary, the Yukon meets its only salt water, the Beaufort Sea. Herschel Island, once an important whaling harbour, lies just off the northern mainland. In its southwestern corner, the Yukon border is only a few kilometres inland from the Gulf of Alaska.

The Yukon is the eighth largest of Canada's territories and provinces. Its land mass is 4.8 percent of the area of the whole country. Yet fewer than 33 000 people live there.

A Rugged Surface

The Yukon is a region of mountains, plains and plateaus separated by large valleys. Its mountains are the northern parts of the Western Cordillera, the vast parallel chains and ranges of mountains that stretch all along the western edge of North America, from Mexico to Alaska.

In the northern and northeastern Yukon lie the Brooks, Mackenzie and Richardson mountains. They are the northern reaches of the Canadian Rockies, the easternmost mountains of the Western Cordillera. They straddle the Yukon–NWT border, curling west through the northern part of the territory. The Brooks Range

Burwash Uplands, Kluane National Park

continues into Alaska. The Yukon's northern and northeastern mountains are not as high as the younger ones of the southwest, and some are very rounded. Many have glaciers.

The Pelly-Cassiar, Ogilvie and Selwyn mountains and the Yukon Plateau lie in the Yukon part of the Western Cordillera region, called the interior. The mountains lie to the west of the Rocky Mountain extensions. The Yukon Plateau, a rolling upland, is a broad diagonal band running northwest into Alaska. It is west of the interior mountains. The Yukon River and its major tributaries, the Pelly and the Stewart rivers, flow through it. The Yukon part of the interior is cut through by two deep geological faults, the Tintina and the Denali. These faults were caused by great stresses in the earth, which created giant cracks in the rock. The two sides of the crack slid sideways along the fault line. The Tintina Trench now looks like a deep valley cutting through the relatively low Yukon Plateau. The Denali Fault divides the Yukon Plateau from the Coast Mountains. It is not as long as the Tintina.

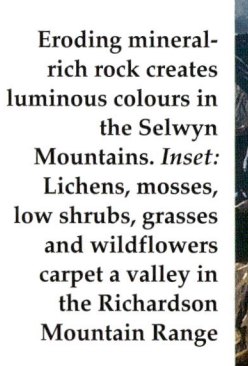

Eroding mineral-rich rock creates luminous colours in the Selwyn Mountains. *Inset:* **Lichens, mosses, low shrubs, grasses and wildflowers carpet a valley in the Richardson Mountain Range**

The Coast Mountains cut through the southwestern part of the territory and continue into Alaska. The mountains are snow-covered all year round; they contain the largest non-polar ice fields in the world because they are so high. The geological forces that created them continue, so they are still rising about two centimetres (less than an inch) a year. The highest mountain in Canada can be found in this range. Formerly, Mount Logan's height had been estimated at between 5951 and 6050 metres (19 524 and 19 849 feet). The year 1992 was the 150th anniversary of the Geological Survey of Canada, Canada's 125th birthday and the 50th anniversary of the building of the Alaska Highway. To honour these events, a team of mountaineers and scientists climbed the mountain. At the top, they measured it using the highly accurate satellite Global Positioning System (GPS). On Canada Day 1992, the mountain was officially declared to be 5959 metres (19 550 feet) high.

Left: **Carcross Desert, known as "the smallest desert in the world," was originally covered by a large glacial lake.** *Right:* **Kaskawulsh Glacier, St. Elias Mountains, Kluane National Park**

Mountaineers at the top of Mt. Logan, Canada's highest peak, during the 1992 anniversary climb to accurately measure its height

A Patchwork of Underlying Rock

The geology of the Yukon is complicated. The rock in the eastern mountains is very different from the rock on the Pacific coast because the Yukon Territory was not created all at once. Plate tectonics is a geological explanation that says the world's continents and ocean bottoms are floating on a layer of molten rock. The earth's spin causes them to move around very slowly and bump into each other. When they bump, one "plate" often slides under another.

On the Pacific coast of North America, for example, the floor of the Pacific Ocean is being pushed under the North American plate. The forces that build up in this process bend and fold the rock above, creating mountains. Sometimes large pieces of rock on a plate do not slide easily under another plate. They get scraped off and stick to the edge of the upper plate. This is what seems to have happened to the ancient edge of North America. Over the last billion years, it has collected huge pieces of rock from other parts of the globe in a process called accretion. That is apparently how the Yukon was formed.

Geologists know for sure that the west coast's huge islands (some, hundreds of kilometres long and wide), called terranes, came from other parts of the world. Each terrane has a "fingerprint." Its

Above: Basaltic rock of Miles Canyon along the Yukon River near Whitehorse. *Left:* The Ogilvie Mountains rise steeply above a river flowing through a broad, flat-bottomed valley in the interior of the Yukon

specific rocks, fossils and chemical makeup can be matched to its parent. Scientists believe they were added to the west coast in two major events. The first occurred about 160 million years ago, the second about 50 million years ago.

The Yukon is a patchwork of very different rocks. Some were formed in volcanoes; others once lay at the bottom of prehistoric oceans. The Mackenzie Mountains in the northeast are composed of the rocks of the ancient North American edge. These rocks are very old, ranging in age from the Late Precambrian (a billion years ago) to the Triassic period (250 million years ago). The geological features lying to the west of the Mackenzies are younger.

Rivers and Lakes

The Yukon River, Canada's second longest, is the only river that is born in a province and flows across a territory and through a state before emptying into the ocean. Its headwaters are in Lake Bennett, in northern British Columbia, only 60 kilometres (37 miles) from the Pacific Ocean. From its source, it twists and turns in a winding

The Yukon is named after its most important river *(right)*, which drains almost two-thirds of the territory. *Above:* Peel River canyon in northeastern Yukon

route for 3185 kilometres (1979 miles) through the Yukon and Alaska before reaching the Bering Sea. In its course through the Yukon Plateau, the Yukon River widens into several large lakes and is joined by several major tributaries. At Nome, Alaska, it forms a huge delta of wide twisting waterways.

The Yukon River is closely linked to the history of the territory. With its main tributaries, the Klondike, Stewart, White, Pelly, Teslin and Takhini, the river was for thousands of years the main route into and through the Yukon and Alaska. Rafts, canoes, boats and sternwheelers all plied its unpredictable waters. Today, while the river is no longer the economic lifeline of the territory, travelling its 650 kilometres (400 miles) between Whitehorse and Dawson is a popular summer adventure.

The Liard River, in the southeast corner of the Yukon, and the Peel, in the northeast, join the Mackenzie River on its journey through the western NWT to the Arctic Ocean. In the northern Yukon, the Porcupine River empties into the Yukon River after it crosses the Alaska border. The Alsek River flows southward through the St. Elias Mountains. It is the only Yukon river that flows directly into the Pacific Ocean. Before the Ice Age, the Yukon River probably emptied into the Pacific, but when ice blocked its path, the river carved its roundabout route to the Bering Sea.

Kluane Lake, the Yukon's largest body of water, is easily accessible through Kluane National Park.

Lake Laberge, north of Whitehorse, was made famous by Robert W. Service in his poem "The Cremation of Sam McGee." It is a large lake and one of several in the Yukon that support small commercial fisheries. Other lakes in the south include Aishihik, Bennett, Dezadeash, Frances, Kluane, Kusawa, Marsh, Tagish and Teslin. There are few large lakes in the interior and northern Yukon because it was not covered during the Ice Age. Most of the large Yukon lakes are quite deep. They rarely warm up enough for swimming except in areas close to shore.

Climate

The Yukon lies in the Subarctic climate zone. Temperatures can range from −40°C (−40°F) or colder to 30°C (86°F) or warmer. The coldest temperature ever recorded in the Yukon was at Snag in the western part of the interior. In February 1947, after weeks of cold, the temperature dipped to −62.8°C (−81°F). The highest temperature on record is 35°C (95°F) at Dawson. The average temperatures are less extreme. For example, in Whitehorse, the territory's capital, the average temperature is −19°C (−2°F) in January and 14°C (57°F) in July.

Winter is the most important season in the North. It is so important to people that they have a joke about there being only two seasons in the Yukon, this winter and last winter. Besides being cold, winters are long and dark. On average, Dawson City's first day of frost is August 27; Whitehorse, 536 kilometres (333 miles) to the south, usually gets its first frost a few days later. In general, across the territory, the average final spring frost occurs in mid-June. Lakes and small rivers can begin to freeze by early October. At midwinter (December 21), the days are at their shortest. Residents of Old Crow do not see daylight at all. Dawson receives only 3.8 hours of sunlight; Whitehorse gets 5.6 hours and Watson Lake 5.7.

The dry climate of the Yukon means that snowfalls are not very heavy. On average, Dawson City receives 136.4 centimetres (53.7 inches) of snow and Whitehorse 127.8 centimetres (50 inches). This is less than most other places in Canada except the west coast of British Columbia and the Arctic Islands of the NWT. There is so

North of Carmacks are the turbulent waters of Five Finger Rapids on the Yukon River. *Below:* Frozen over approximately six months of each year. *Below right:* In summer. *Inset:* Whitehorse in January with the temperature at -48°C (-54°F). Cars are left with their motors running for the entire church

little snow that, in most communities, the main roads are not ploughed. Instead, vehicles driving on the roads pack the snow down. Gravel is put down at intersections to give tires enough added grip to stop. Winter can affect driving in other ways. When it is very cold, cars can develop "square wheels." This happens when the car is standing overnight and the tires freeze. The part of the tire that is on the ground develops a flat spot that lasts until the tire warms up. Driving on frozen tires is a bumpy experience.

Yukon summers are short but generally pleasant. Temperatures regularly reach the mid-twenties (70°F). On midsummer day, June 21, Old Crow receives 24 hours of sun, Dawson City almost 21, Whitehorse and Watson 19. Through most of the territory, the twilight lingers almost to sunrise, making it possible to read outside at midnight. From this comes the nickname "Land of the Midnight Sun."

Permafrost and Northern Lights

In the Yukon, permafrost is a problem for gardeners as well as builders. Permafrost is frozen ground that never thaws. It occurs in scattered pockets in the south and everywhere in the north. The ground is frozen anywhere from 10 centimetres (4 inches) to 30 centimetres (12 inches) below the surface, and the frost can be more than 300 metres (almost 1000 feet) deep. (Permafrost can even be found under the Arctic Ocean).

In the summer, the top layer, called the active layer, melts. In the flat tundra areas of the northern Yukon, the resulting water cannot drain away. It simply stays on the ground, providing excellent breeding areas for billions of flies and mosquitoes. For gardeners and farmers, permafrost can mean stunted plants and low yields because roots cannot grow deep enough to develop a big plant. Builders have problems with permafrost because heat from house foundations and road beds causes the permafrost to melt. Things built on the frozen ground begin to sink or tilt. In some places people use holes dug in the permafrost as refrigerators.

One of nature's most extravagant wonders, the aurora borealis, or northern lights, in the night skies above Whitehorse. Caused by electromagnetic activity among air molecules, streams and bands of glowing green, red and purple light swirl in the sky.

The northern lights, or aurora borealis, are a truly northern phenomenon. They can be seen all winter long, but particularly on clear nights in the late fall and early spring. The sky seems filled with swaying streamers of pale light. The green, pink or blue streamers arch and dance across the sky, fading and returning, waving like curtains. The aurora occurs when electrically charged particles are blown out from the sun by solar winds. These particles become trapped by the earth's magnetic field and come into contact with the gases making up the atmosphere. The gas molecules become charged and glow like neon lights. Scientists are certain the lights make no noise, but some northerners swear they crackle and that the air vibrates. (The northern lights are occasionally seen in southern Canada, but their displays are not nearly as dramatic as they are in the North.)

Trees and Forests

Boreal forest covers 281 000 square kilometres (108 500 square miles), or about 58 percent of the Yukon. Freshwater lakes and rivers cover 4480 square kilometres (1730 square miles), or just under one percent of the land mass. The remaining part includes the area above the tree line, and the tundra and bog vegetation of the North.

Pine and white and black spruce are the most common evergreen

Evergreen forest at the treeline, north of the Arctic Circle. *Inset:* Mountainsides and valleys are covered with the shimmering gold of aspens in early September.

trees in the territory. Most of the Yukon's deciduous trees are birch and poplar. Tamaracks (northern larch) are found in the southeast. All trees grow slowly in the thin soil, long winters and short summers. They are generally smaller than those in southern Canada.

Fire is an important part of the Yukon's forest ecosystem. Fires started randomly by lightning strikes burn a given area in a 30- to 100-year cycle.

Yukon wildlife benefits from the periodic renewal of the forests. Dense forests are unsuitable habitats for many of the larger animals because lack of sunlight means little grows at ground level. Soon after a fire, the first plants begin to grow and pine cones, baked in the fire, open to spread their seeds. Animals, attracted to the tender young plants, move into the area again. In the difficult northern environment, however, a forest will take 100 years or more to mature.

Lightning- and people-caused fires are a seasonal threat to communities and businesses. During the summer, fire-fighters remain on alert, prepared to move out at a moment's notice to fight blazes that endanger Yukon highways or communities. Forest fires can have some strange benefits for people, however. A huge fire that burned to the outskirts of Whitehorse in 1958 has provided thousands with excellent winter firewood ever since. The trees left standing with their bark burned off are "air dried" and very good for burning.

Flowers and Berries

An estimated 1300 species of wildflowers, ferns and shrubs flourish across the territory. They grow well in the valleys and on south-facing slopes. Even the high country, well above the tree line, has beautiful meadows and small pockets of wildflowers.

In spring, the pasque flower, or Yukon crocus, with its fragile lavender petals, is the first to push through the melting snow. By early summer, Yukon roadsides are lined with masses of purple vetch and blue Jacob's ladder. Blue lupins carpet the forests.

Fireweed, the Yukon's official flower, is the first plant to flourish in burned or cleared areas. Its tall magenta flowers often line the sides of highways with colour. The bright primary shades of arctic

Fireweed in the fall along North Canol Road in the Mackenzie Mountain Range. *Right:* **Wildflowers growing in a burned-out tree stump.** *Far right:* **Poppy garden near the Yukon-Alaska border**

poppies are everywhere. Every open space has its own flower community, be it bog or tundra, mountain slope or forest glade. Meadows of white, fluffy arctic cotton grass cover the swampy tundra in summer. Wild roses, wild sweet peas, marsh marigolds, violets, furry pussy paws, mountain avens, shooting stars, saxifrage, anemones, columbines, tiny pink twinflowers and even small orchids flourish. However, most flowers and other plants are slower growing and smaller than similar ones in southern Canada.

Wild berries are prized by people and animals for their sweetness. A homemade mossberry pie is a special Yukon delicacy, and soapberries are important to bears as they store up fat for winter hibernation. Like the flowers, the berries tend to be smaller than those in the south, but they are bursting with flavour. Yukon berry species include kinnickinnick or bearberry, crowberry (mossberry), low and high bush cranberry, blueberry, strawberry, raspberry, cloudberry and soapberry.

Far left: Arctic cotton covers the swampy tundra in summer. *Left:* Squirreltail grass near the abandoned village of Champagne. *Below:* Kinnickinnick, or bearberry, one of the surviving berry plants in the Carcross Desert

Wildlife

The Yukon is the last frontier for many animals. Grizzly and black bears, moose and caribou, Dall's and stone sheep, wolves, foxes and coyotes roam at will across the territory. Mule deer and cougars are less common but appear to be moving in from the south, and small herds of elk and wood bison have been imported in the hope of increasing their numbers. Many smaller animals also live in the Yukon. They include ground squirrels, hoary marmots, red squirrels, porcupines, beavers, wolverines and minks. Chipmunks and pikas are seen in some areas. Polar bears, whales, seals and walruses are found in the far north around Herschel Island.

Caribou have always been particularly important to First Nations people, who hunted — and still hunt — them for food and skins. Today, the Porcupine River barren-ground caribou herd numbers about 245 000 animals. Following the same migratory pattern it

Stone sheep *(below)* and Dall's sheep *(far right)* live on the steep mountainsides foraging for mosses, wildflowers and hardy grasses. *Right:* Porcupine caribou herds roam the northern coastal plain between Old Crow and the sea, wintering in the Yukon and migrating in the spring to their calving grounds in Alaska.

used in the distant past, this herd ranges over the northern coastal plain through the north Yukon's mountainous regions and into eastern Alaska. Woodland (mountain) caribou are scattered in small herds throughout the central and southern Yukon. There are an estimated 28 000 animals in 20 herds of varying sizes.

Predatory birds found in the Yukon include bald eagles, golden eagles, owls, hawks, peregrines and gyrfalcons. Game birds such as grouse and ptarmigans are plentiful. Waterfowl include Canada geese, swans, loons and many kinds of ducks. Ravens and jays, sparrows and swallows, larks and bluebirds and even chickadees live in the Yukon. Migratory birds are attracted north to nest every year by the large numbers of insects that form the main part of their food during the breeding season.

Fish found in Yukon waters include rainbow trout, lake trout, brook trout, arctic char, Dolly Varden, squanga whitefish, ling cod, jackfish, grayling, inconnu, pike and salmon. Salmon have long been an important staple for residents of the territory. The First Nations people maintained traditional fish camps, where fish were netted, gaffed or trapped. Chinook, chum, sockeye and coho are the most numerous species of salmon in the Yukon.

Far left: **Boreal owl with its prey.**
Left: **Grizzly bears are found almost everywhere in the Yukon. Kluane National Park has the largest concentration of these huge animals.**

CHAPTER 3

First Peoples

The origins of the Yukon's first inhabitants still present major questions for anthropologists and archaeologists. The First Nations have had their own explanations for thousands of years. Their oral traditions say that Raven stole light and illuminated the earth. He created water, land and the animals. He found the first people in a clamshell on a beach, and so the world was peopled.

Theories put forward by anthropologists and archaeologists are less poetic and involve migrations from Asia over a land bridge that existed many thousands of years ago. The earliest actual evidence of human activity in the territory comes from the Bluefish caves south of Old Crow in the northern Yukon, where bones of animals discarded by hunters have been found. According to scientists, these bones date back between 12 000 and 24 000 years. Northern climate conditions make it difficult to date these finds more precisely.

Languages and Lifeways

Today the Yukon First Nations may be divided into two main language groups. Most speak one or more of the Athapaskan languages, which include Gwich'in (or Kutchin), Han, Northern and Southern Tutchone, Kaska and Tagish (now extinct). The Athapaskan languages of the Yukon First Nations are distantly related to each other. Thousands of years of living in different areas, however, mean that the languages are not similar now, and a speaker of one cannot understand a speaker of another. The second

Gwich'in hunters. The Gwich'in were — and are — the northernmost of the Yukon First Nations.

main language group is Tlingit. Tlingit speakers from the west coast migrated inland and settled in the southern part of the territory.

Until the mid-1800s, a small number of Inuit also lived in the Yukon, on the north coast. Unfortunately, they were decimated by diseases introduced by American whalers who began operating in the area in the 1890s. Today Inuvialuit (Western Arctic Inuit) visit the north coast of the Yukon for hunting, but do not live there permanently.

The traditional lifeways of the different Yukon First Nations had — and have — many features in common. Each used specific resources, but all organized their lives according to a seasonal pattern. The Subarctic is a harsh environment. A group of people could not stay put and hope to find all they needed to survive. Certain resources were more abundant in some places and at some times of the year. Thus the people would move from one camp to another to take advantage of this.

In the summer, the people would gather in quite large numbers at fish camps. Men set and cleared the willow traps and nets or used bone hooks and spears to catch fish. Women cleaned, prepared and dried the fish for winter. The people harvested a variety of plants including berries, mosses and barks, and snared small animals such as hares and rabbits. The fish camps were also places to trade with the Tlingit people of the coast, who brought shells, eulachon (candlefish) oil, wooden boxes and dried foods. The Tlingit left with such trade items as hides, dried meat, raw copper and mountain goat hair.

In the fall, the group would disperse to hunt big game. In some areas hunters built caribou traps. These were like huge funnels with a fenced corral at the narrow end. Hunters herded caribou into the corral, where other hunters waited for them. The women cut up the meat and prepared the hides for tanning. The people had a use for every part of the animal, from the horns to the hoofs, to the bones and intestines. The body of one caribou could provide scrapers, needles, weapons, tools, sinew for sewing, cord for snowshoes, hide

Top: For Yukon Native peoples, the caribou was an all-important source of food and of skins for clothing and shelter. On the open tundra, hunters often drove the animals between two long rows of poles into a corral, where many could be quickly killed. *Bottom:* Women preparing caribou skins, which they will later cut and sew into shirts or moccasins or other articles of clothing

for clothing and lots of meat, of course. When the hunt was good, there would be feasting. Meat not eaten right way was dried or smoked for winter. Besides caribou, the peoples of the Yukon also hunted a variety of other animals and birds. Depending on their location, these included mountain goats, Dall's sheep, moose, beavers, bears, ducks and geese. The hunters used bows and arrows, as well as snaring techniques.

In the winter, the people lived near lakes in fairly small groups because it was easier to feed a small group than a big one. For fresh food they snared small animals and fished through holes in the ice. As long as the food lasted, the group stayed together in one place. In late winter, when supplies began running low, members of the group would go off to look for beavers, muskrat, rabbits and fish.

Spring was the hardest season because melting ice and snow made travel difficult and dangerous. Animals that had survived the winter were thin. Salmon had not yet returned from the ocean to spawn. Plants and berries had still not appeared. For the people, it was a struggle to survive a bit longer until they could again meet at the fish camps.

The Yukon First Nations mostly travelled their seasonal round on foot. They used snowshoes in winter. Women hauled the food and gear on hide toboggans and in packsacks. In summer the people occasionally travelled in canoes made of cedar bark, birch bark or moose hide. People in the southern part of the Yukon made dugouts of local spruce or cottonwood. Temporary rafts were used everywhere for short trips.

Like other Native peoples, Yukon First Nations had strong spiritual beliefs that required them to show respect for all things in nature. Singing, drumming and dancing were all part of their way of honouring the spirits of the animals and plants that made life possible for them.

The First Nations were at home on the land. They understood its rhythms and its ways. Their stories, handed from one generation to another, held the wisdom of many, many generations. Knowledge and skill were vital in a lifeway that demanded the people move most of the time. A person who could readily make what was needed did not have to carry it along. The importance of knowledge and skill was well understood, and contained in the oral traditions of the people.

Trade Networks

Before the First Nations had direct contact with non-Natives, they had established extensive trade networks. The Yukon First Nations traded with each other and with other peoples whose territories bordered theirs.

The Tlingit-speaking coastal peoples controlled the mountain passes to the Yukon interior. With the arrival of Russians in Alaska, the Chilkat Tlingit of the Haines area of Alaska became intermediaries in trade. The Yukon First Nations dealt almost

These Gwich'in men have obviously been trading with Europeans, since one now carries a gun and powder horn. In fact, the picture was drawn by Hudson's Bay Company trader Alexander Murray, who established Fort Yukon in 1847.

exclusively with the Chilkat for Russian and other European trade goods. In time the Chilkat monopoly was broken by the arrival of Hudson's Bay Company explorers and traders, many of them British.

The arrival of European fur traders in the Yukon did not alter the lifeways of the Yukon people a great deal. They continued their seasonal rounds, adapting their hunting to obtain the furs that the traders wanted. Unlike the First Nations in other parts of Canada, they did not move into camps around trading posts, nor did they become fulltime hunters for the posts. The First Nations peoples of the Yukon retained control in trading: if the goods offered them or the prices were not acceptable, they simply refused to trade. When the Hudson's Bay Company lost interest in trading in the area and abandoned its posts, the First Nations peoples returned to their traditional lifeways. By this time, however, these ways had been altered to some extent by the introduction of metal pots, flour, cloth, guns and other European trade goods. Their numbers had also been seriously affected by the introduction of European diseases such as measles, smallpox and influenza.

Changes: Wages, Schools and a Highway

By the 1870s prospectors, too, had begun trickling into the Yukon, but for a time they were too few in number to have any real impact. It was the gold rush of 1897-98 that brought the Yukon to world notice and that marked the beginning of major changes for the First Nations. During these years, Yukon Native people first experienced working for wages. They worked as hunters and guides in prospectors' camps. They worked as deckhands and pilots on the riverboats, chopping wood along the way for the steam engines. Some, like "Skookum Jim," one of the original discoverers of Klondike gold, worked their own gold claims.

In the years following the gold rush, life for the First Nations people returned to something close to what it had been

Students and teachers outside the residential school for Native children at Carcross, 1921. Seen with them on the right is Bishop Isaac Stringer.

traditionally. Some people chose to live in or near Dawson, Mayo and Whitehorse, doing whatever work they could find. Others returned to the land and made their living hunting and trapping as their ancestors had done.

Some things had changed. Christian missionaries, (mostly Anglicans,) now worked regularly among the First Nations. The church set up day schools in some areas to teach the Native people reading, arithmetic and other subjects. Later a boarding school was built at Carcross. The education young Native people received at the school made it difficult for them to return home. The school had given them ideas different from those of their parents. They were no longer comfortable with their own culture but were not at ease in the new Canadian one either. Beginning in the 1940s, First Nations students began to attend regular public schools. In the 1960s the boarding school finally closed.

During the building of the Alaska Highway in 1942, some First Nations men worked as guides and suppliers. Women sold food and crafts to the military and civilian highway workers. The completed highway brought more changes to the lives of the southern First Nations peoples. The Kaska, Inland Tlingit, Tagish and Southern Tutchone were soon drawn into new communities along the highway. They moved into such places as Watson Lake, Teslin, Champagne, Haines Junction, Destruction Bay and Beaver Creek.

Land Claims

Today the Yukon First Nations are organized in bands. The bands represent people who live in and use traditional areas of the territory.

Elijah Smith founded the Yukon Native Brotherhood in 1969. The Brotherhood began working to get the government to agree to settle their land claims. Unlike First Nations peoples in some other parts of Canada, the Yukon First Nations never signed a treaty giving up any of their land to the Canadian government. They want control over how natural resources are used, as well as other matters relating to their land and lives. In 1973 the Brotherhood published a statement about their claim called *Together Today for Our Children Tomorrow*. The Yukon land claim may become a model for other similar claims around the world.

Negotiations between the federal government and the new Council for Yukon Indians (CYI) began and broke off several times. One agreement was rejected by the First Nations in 1984. A new round of talks began three years later, and in 1991 an agreement between the CYI, the federal government and the Yukon government was signed. It was called an umbrella agreement because it applied to all the bands. It was not the final agreement. It outlined the procedures and ideas for that final agreement. The umbrella agreement gave 8.6 percent of the Yukon (41 439 square kilometres, or 16 000 square miles) to the First Nations. The 14 bands have to decide which lands each wants to control. Land will be chosen for its hunting, fishing, trapping and spiritual importance. The First Nations will also receive about $246.6 million to run their own local housing, education and health programs.

A second umbrella agreement was signed by four of the 14 bands in May 1993. The federal minister of Indian Affairs and Northern Development, Tom Siddon, and the Yukon government leader, John

A few of the Yukon's First Nations people today

Ostashek, signed for the governments. This agreement allows each band to form its own local government and sets aside 12 percent of the Yukon for the First Nations. The first four bands to sign were the Champagne-Aishihik, Nacho Ny'ak Dun, Teslin-Tlingit Council and the Vuntut Gwitch'in.

CHAPTER 4

Fur Traders and Gold-Seekers

The first non-Native person to see any part of the Yukon was Vitus Bering, a Dane working for the Russian navy. Bering was exploring the Gulf of Alaska on July 29, 1741 (St. Elias Day), when he spied the high mountains of the southwest Yukon. He named the highest peak he saw St. Elias Mountain in honour of the saint. The narrow strait separating Siberia and Alaska, only 64 kilometres (40 miles) in width, was later named for Vitus Bering.

Russian fur traders followed Bering to the area. Being mainly interested in sea otter pelts, they kept to the coastal areas. Some of the trade goods made their way inland to the Yukon, but it is doubtful if any Russian actually set foot there. Thus, the Russian presence did not greatly affect the Yukon First Nations. For over a hundred years, Russia traded with Alaskan Native peoples and governed the area. Then, in 1867, it sold Alaska to the United States for $7.2 million.

Trading Posts and Missionaries

The first non-aboriginal fur traders to enter the Yukon worked for the Hudson's Bay Company (HBC), whose headquarters were in London, England. The first Hudson's Bay Company explorers and traders arrived in 1840. They were looking for new places to build trading posts, from which to obtain furs from the Native peoples. However, the people of the Mackenzie Valley would not let the traders into the Yukon. They wanted to continue to control the trade, as the Chilkat had with the Russians.

A prospector and his dog

Fort Yukon in June 1867, shortly before American protests that the fort was in their newly acquired territory forced the Hudson's Bay Company to close it.

Robert Campbell was a clerk with the HBC. Sent to explore routes into the Yukon from the south, he established the first post in 1842 at Fort Frances in the southeast part of the territory. Campbell stayed at Fort Frances for a year or so, then continued his survey of the area and founded Fort Selkirk at the junction of the Yukon and Pelly rivers. The post lasted only four years; it was burned down in 1852 by a party of Chilkat.

John Bell was another HBC explorer. Having found a way over the mountains from the Mackenzie Valley, he reached the Porcupine River and followed it into Alaska, where it joins the great Yukon River. Bell heard the local Gwich'in people's name for this river. To him it sounded like Yukon, so that became the name in English, both for the river and eventually the territory.

Another HBC man, Alexander Hunter Murray, set up Fort Yukon in the area in 1847. The post saw many years of active and profitable trade. After 1867, however, American traders complained that Fort Yukon was in Alaska, which the United States had just bought from Russia, and the HBC was forced to move it. Several moves later, the post was finally on Canadian soil, but it did not continue to do well. Part of the reason was competition from American traders. At last the HBC decided to abandon its Yukon trade.

Far left: **Anglican bishop William C. Bompas helping to work a raft. Bishop Bompas spent over 40 years in the Canadian North, many of them in the Yukon.** *Left:* **Bompas' wife, Charlotte Selina, worked with him to educate Yukon Natives in European ways and the Christian religion. She is seen here with one of many sick or orphaned children she cared for in her home.**

Anglican missionaries began arriving in the 1860s. They spent their time learning the Athapaskan languages and teaching some of the people the Christian faith, as well as reading, arithmetic and other school subjects. Some aboriginal people from other parts of the Northwest helped them by translating and teaching. At first, the missionaries did not have much success. The Yukon First Nations moved around too much for their teaching to be very effective.

Spying Out the Land

By the 1870s, a small number of miners and prospectors were in the Yukon. Some had taken part in the gold rushes in California (1848) and British Columbia (1860s). They were sure there had to be lots of gold in the Yukon as well. Some of the miners travelled up the Liard River into the Yukon. Others journeyed over the Chilkoot Pass from the Pacific coast near Skagway, Alaska. They travelled down the Yukon River and prospected along the way.

George Holt was probably the first non-Native to cross the Chilkoot Pass. Historians believe he made the crossing in 1878. The Chilkoot, Chilkat and other coastal peoples controlled the pass and thus trade with the interior. They did not want anyone else to use it. A small group of prospectors later fired a machine gun loaded with blanks, forcing the local people to let them cross. In the years that followed, many gold-seekers entered the Yukon over this pass.

Surveyors also began to take an interest in the Yukon. In 1883 Lieutenant Frederick Schwatka of the United States Army led a survey group across the Chilkoot Pass and down the Yukon River. Schwatka did not do much actual surveying. His purpose was to assess the military value of the Yukon River basin. He did, however, give English names to many of the mountains, lakes and rivers that he saw. Some of Schwatka's names are now official. Others were later changed.

George Dawson was the assistant director of the Geological Survey of Canada. In 1887 he led one of three survey groups in an expedition to study the geology of the Yukon. Dawson's group travelled along "rivers, lakes and portages of the interior ... the total distance traversed being about 1322 miles" (2127 kilometres). On the journey, they studied the geology, plants, animals and people of the territory. In his report, Dawson wrote that he thought substantial amounts of gold would soon be found in the Yukon.

Although no major gold discovery occurred immediately, mining activity increased in the Yukon. Steamers sailed up and down the Pacific coast from May to October. They brought in miners, mail and supplies, and took miners and mail back out again. The Alaska Commercial Company had several steamers travelling regularly up and down the Yukon River between Nome and Circle City. Other boats continued on to the little mining settlement at Fortymile in the Yukon, where the company had set up a small supply post. Fortymile, about 75 kilometres (46 miles) downriver from Dawson, was where most of the mining was going on at the time.

In the absence of any established civil authority, the miners made their own rules. They set up a system of miners' meetings to deal with problems. Any person with a complaint could call a meeting. For example, one miner might accuse another of stealing his food supplies. All the miners would hear the complaint, and then they would listen to the accused person. Finally they would discuss the problem until they came to a solution. Sometimes the offending person would be exiled from the community. This was the most serious punishment, since there were so few people in the area and they needed each other's help.

Law and Order

The activity in the Yukon had not gone unnoticed by the Canadian government. Officials had had complaints that American and Canadian miners were fighting over gold claims near Dawson. Bishop William C. Bompas, an Anglican missionary in the area, wrote to Ottawa in 1893. He complained that the miners were giving alcohol to the local people.

The federal government decided it was time to pay more attention to this remote part of its vast North-West Territories (which at the time included most of today's Prairie provinces as well as the present-day Northwest Territories). It feared that the United States might claim the Yukon because there were so many Americans

By the time eager gold-seekers began pouring into the Yukon by the thousands, the Royal Canadian Mounted Police had established their authority in Dawson and at the main points of entry into the territory.

there. In 1894, Inspector Charles Constantine and Staff-Sergeant Charles Brown of the North West Mounted Police (now the Royal Canadian Mounted Police) were sent to investigate the situation.

Constantine returned to Ottawa and reported that large quantities of supplies were being brought into the Yukon from the United States, and no customs duties were being collected. He also said that people were not paying taxes on the gold they were mining. This was not surprising because there was no Canadian official there to collect them. Constantine recommended that a detachment of 40 North West Mounted Police (NWMP) be sent to the Yukon. The government sent him back in 1895 with 19 men. This small group was to bring law and order to the Yukon District.

The NWMP soon took over from the miners, enforcing the law of Canada regarding stealing and other crimes. They also had many other duties as, in effect, they were the government in the region. They collected taxes, ran the mail service, and acted as land and gold agents. They took on the roles of judges, welfare workers and health officers.

From some of the discoveries prospectors were making, the police were convinced that a rich gold strike was going to happen soon. Since this would bring many more people into the area, Constantine asked the government to send more men. In 1897 the police force was doubled, and its headquarters were set up in Dawson.

The Gold Rush

In August 1896, a Californian named George Carmack, his Tagish wife, Kate, and her brothers "Skookum Jim" and "Tagish Charlie" discovered large nuggets of gold on Rabbit Creek, near Dawson. Rabbit Creek was a tributary of a river that the local people called the Throndiuk. English-speaking newcomers, mispronouncing the name, called it the Klondike. This name was soon to echo around the world, starting the great Klondike Gold Rush.

George Carmack, who started the rush for gold, as portrayed on the front of the first issue of the *Klondike News*

    Shortly after George Carmack began prospecting in the area, he met a Nova Scotian, Robert Henderson, who had been in the region for about two years. Henderson told him of several creeks he should look at, and Carmack promised to tell Henderson if he found anything. At a later meeting, Henderson was rude to Carmack's Tagish wife and her brothers. He made it clear that he didn't want any "Siwashes" (Native people) staking gold claims in the area. Not surprisingly Carmack took offence, and when he and his group made their big discovery, they did not tell Henderson.
    By the time Robert Henderson arrived at Rabbit Creek, which had been renamed Bonanza Creek, miners from the Fortymile area had already staked most of its richest claims. They thawed and dug gravel during the winter. In the spring, they cleaned up the gold. They packed it in jam jars and coffee tins and sailed away to Portland and Seattle. A newspaper headline announced that one

ship had a "ton of gold" on board. Almost immediately eager gold-seekers — Americans, Canadians, Europeans and others — began planning to go to the Klondike. The world had been in an economic recession. People were tired of bad times. The Klondike seemed to promise a chance to get rich quickly.

Doctors and clerks, farmers and printers, miners and ministers, men and women dropped everything and headed for Seattle and Victoria. Some changed their minds before they boarded the boats. Others lost everything to criminals in Skagway. Still others lost hope when they saw the Chilkoot Pass or had their boats or rafts fall apart in the Yukon River Rapids. Many, however — 30 000 to 40 000 — made it to Dawson City, only to discover that the best spots along the gold creeks had already been staked. Some left immediately. Others stayed and started restaurants, shops, saloons and dance halls.

Some of the gold stampeders used the "all-Canadian Route" from Edmonton. This route followed the rivers and lakes used by the early fur traders. It had the advantage of Hudson's Bay posts along part of the way, where would-be miners could buy supplies. The route was difficult, however. Of the 2000 or so who tried it, many turned back, and almost 500 died on the way. It took the few who made it to Dawson two years to get there.

For gold-seekers arriving by way of the port of Skagway, the route to the goldfields lay over one of two mountain passes. These were the White Pass and the Chilkoot Pass in the Alaska Panhandle. There was some dispute over the location of the Canada–United States border at the time. Determined to establish its authority over all who attempted to cross these passes, the Canadian government ordered Superintendent Samuel Steele of the North West Mounted Police to set up a post at the summit of Chilkoot Pass. The NWMP were to ensure that customs duties were paid on all American goods brought into Canada and that each person entering the Yukon had enough supplies to last a year (about 1000 kilograms/2200 pounds). This action secured the

Getting there was definitely not "half the fun" — in fact it was not fun at all. Seen here, *clockwise from top left:* **Women prospectors were few, but they were determined; climbing the "Golden Stairs" to the summit of the Chilkoot Pass; boat building at Lake Bennett; shooting the rapids at Miles Canyon, just south of Whitehorse.**

summit as Canadian soil. It also saved many lives. The tiny communities at Fortymile and Dawson were unprepared for the stampeders. No matter how much money — or gold — a person had, there was little in the way of food and supplies to buy, especially at the beginning.

Between the fall of 1897 and the spring of 1898, 22 000 stampeders struggled through the deep snow of the 1122-metre (3680-foot) Chilkoot Pass under the watchful eye of the NWMP. Each person had to make an average of 30 trips to bring the required "ton of goods" to the summit. Tea and coffee, salt and sugar, boots and beans, lamps and lard, needles and thread, picks and shovels were pulled on sleds or carried on the backs of people or animals. Stairs were cut into the snow to make the climb a bit easier, but as the endless line of gold-seekers staggered up the 1500 steps, there was no room for mistakes. If a person fell or stopped to rest, it might take hours to get back in line.

Dogs were in high demand for pulling sleds and carrying packs of supplies. Indirectly, the price they fetched got the Yukon its first effective commissioner. In the fall of 1896, William Ogilvie of the Geological Survey of Canada missed the last boat out of Dawson to Whitehorse. When he found it would cost him $1000 for a dog team to get him out, he decided to stay. He began an official survey of the gold fields. His work and his fair dealing with the miners earned him widespread respect and admiration.

Stampeders who thought that their troubles were over once they had made it to the summit of the Chilkoot and the shores of Lindeman Lake soon found out they were wrong. The next task for many was to build a boat that could carry them and their supplies to Dawson as soon as the ice on the lakes and the Yukon River broke up. Many stampeders had never handled tools of any kind. Their boats needed to be strong enough to carry heavy loads and to withstand the rapids of the Yukon River. Soon the gold-seekers had cut down all the trees around the lake.

Enough people built boats that, when the ice was finally gone, thousands set sail for Dawson. Each boat was stopped and numbered as it passed the NWMP detachment at Tagish. The police also recorded the names of the people in the boats so that they could check later and make sure that those on board had actually made it to Dawson. There were many hazards along the way.

About 150 boats sank in the Whitehorse Rapids in one season. Amazingly, most of the overloaded, jerry-built little craft and their passengers did reach Dawson.

Life in "The Paris of the North"

By June 1898, Dawson City had a population of 30 000 or more. No one bothered to count all the people. Most were too busy looking for gold. In no time 500 buildings were crammed onto a small gravel bank at the mouth of the Klondike River. All kinds of businesses were set up in log huts and in tents. Dawson began

Panning was one way of separating gold particles from the dirt and gravel of stream beds. A system of sluice boxes, which could handle a lot more gravel a lot faster, was another. Both required a great deal of back-breaking digging — a task not made any pleasanter by the Yukon's voracious mosquito population.

Clockwise from left: It is said that prospectors' habit of paying their bills with gold dust created a side industry in Dawson — panning spilled dust from the floors of saloons; Dawson in its bustling, boisterous heyday; "Tagish Charlie," shortly after his Bonanza Creek claim made him a wealthy man; in most cases, any fortunes the miners gained disappeared quickly into the pockets of saloon keepers, professional gamblers and dancehall girls. As one miner put it, "If you have money, spend it; that's what it's for."

calling itself "The Paris of the North." It was the largest city north of San Francisco and west of Winnipeg. It soon had theatres, saloons, gambling halls, a bank, churches, a hospital, restaurants, general stores and real estate agents. Steamers, stagecoaches and sleds came and went, depending on the season. The sad truth was that more people made fortunes from supplying the miners, "mining the miners," than from actually mining the creeks.

The presence of the police in Dawson kept crime low from the beginning. By early 1898, the NWMP had a force of more than 200 officers and men at posts around the territory. Most were stationed in Dawson. Guns were not allowed in the city, and the police acted quickly to make sure wrongdoers were brought to justice. One of the common sentences, a practical one, was cutting wood for the police detachment. In more severe cases, the criminal was forced to leave Dawson. The community had only a small jail, and there was no way to keep a prisoner for long.

Left: **Samuel Benfield Steele**, commanding officer of the North West Mounted Police, soon become known as the "Lion of the Yukon" for the firmness with which he imposed the law on the rowdy hordes of adventurers who flooded into the Klondike.
Right: The Mounties did not work alone. To strengthen Canadian presence in the Yukon, some 200 volunteers from the Canadian Army, known as the Yukon Field Force, were sent to the territory in 1898. Seen here is the last guard parading at Dawson on June 6, 1900, before the force was withdrawn and replaced by local militia.

Mail and news were important in Dawson during the gold rush. People who received letters would often read them out loud to large groups. Dawson's most famous letter carrier was "The Iron Man," Percy deWolfe. He arrived in Dawson in 1898 and decided to stay. For the next 35 years, deWolfe regularly carried the mail between Dawson and Eagle, Alaska, a distance of 168 kilometres (104 miles). It was an eight-day round trip and nothing stopped him. He travelled by dog team in winter and by boat in summer. Today an annual dog sled race is named for him. The race follows deWolfe's original mail route.

The NWMP continued to carry the mail between Skagway and Dawson. The first mail run into Dawson was by police dog team.

The dog sleds travelled between 60 and 90 kilometres (37 and 56 miles) a day. The run from Skagway (920 kilometres/572 miles) usually took 10 days. In summer the mail was carried by steam-powered paddlewheelers to Whitehorse or to Nome. People leaving the Klondike often charged a dollar each to take letters and mail them in Skagway or in the South.

The Klondike Gold Rush lasted less than five years. Few of the thousands who stampeded into the Yukon in search of a fortune actually found one. Some of those who did kept their new-found wealth. Many gambled or drank their fortunes away. Others left to try their luck in new gold strikes in Alaska and British Columbia.

The Alaska Boundary Dispute

The discovery of gold in the Klondike turned the unsettled Alaska boundary question into a major issue between the American and Canadian governments. The Canadian government argued that a treaty signed in 1825 between Russia and Britain gave Canada important harbours on the ocean inlets of the Alaska Panhandle. The United States, on the other hand, claimed that the Panhandle boundary as vaguely described in the treaty lay farther east and that all access to the coast north of latitude 54° 40' was in their territory.

In 1903 a commission consisting of three Americans, an Englishman and two Canadians was set up to re-examine the 1825 treaty and settle the matter. While the commission was meeting in London, England, American President Theodore Roosevelt was talking about using the army if the United States did not get "satisfaction." In the end, the British delegate refused to risk what he called an "international calamity" and voted with the Americans in support of the United States' claim.

CHAPTER 5
New Transportation and a New North

The Klondike Gold Rush prompted new developments in transportation in the Yukon. Aware of the vast numbers of men and women struggling over the Chilkoot Pass, a group of business people financed a 178-kilometre (110-mile) narrow-gauge railway between Skagway and Whitehorse.

Railway Ties, Sternwheelers and Stagecoaches

More than 2000 men, armed only with picks, shovels and black powder, worked for a year and a half to cut the railway through the White Pass and on to Whitehorse. The track reached the summit (884 metres/2900 feet) in February 1899, and the White Pass and Yukon Railway was completed on July 29, 1900. There was a special ceremony at Carcross to hammer in the last spike holding the track to the ties.

The new railway improved the movement of goods, services and people within as well as into the Yukon. For example, the small freight boats that travelled between Whitehorse and Dawson could not handle the vast amount of cargo very well. Seizing the opportunity, the railway company expanded into river transportation. It started a separate company, the British Yukon Navigation Company (BYNC), which began building sternwheelers at shipyards in Whitehorse and Dawson.

The White Pass and Yukon Railway soon began to carry the mail in the territory. Sternwheelers and stagecoaches were used in the

A remarkable engineering feat when it was built, the White Pass and Yukon Railway was, for a time, the territory's chief employer. Today, it runs only as a tourist attraction.

Right: **Dawson waterfront, 1900.**
Below: **The White Pass and Yukon Railway bridge at Carcross in 1900, shortly after it was completed**

summer. The boats burned about 150 cords of wood on each round trip, and woodcutters were busy maintaining huge piles of wood at refuelling stops along the river. In winter stagecoaches were placed on runners and pulled by teams of six horses each. The first overland stage to Dawson left Whitehorse in November 1902, carrying mail and passengers. The passengers wrapped themselves in buffalo robes to keep warm. The stage stopped regularly at roadhouses, spaced about 32 kilometres (20 miles) apart, to change horses and to allow passengers to eat and rest. It ran regular trips between Dawson and Whitehorse year-round. The trips were

Much of the Yukon, of course, remained beyond the reach of the railway and the sternwheelers. The NWMP, therefore, continued to cover huge distances by dogteam, carrying mail and supplies to its far-flung posts and visiting remote communities along the way. Seen here is the 1909 Dawson to Herschel Island patrol. *Inset:* Inspector Francis Fitzgerald, leader of the famous "lost patrol" — the one tragically unsuccessful episode in the force's remarkable record of patrolling the North. In January 1911, Fitzgerald and his party of three constables lost their way between Fort McPherson and Dawson and starved to death. A search party led by Corporal W.J. Dempster, for whom the highway was later named, found their bodies a few weeks later.

cancelled only when the temperature dropped below –40°C (–40°F) or when the ice on the rivers was not yet thick enough or was beginning to break up.

When the gold rush in the Klondike ended, many stampeders who had staked Yukon claims sold them to large mining companies. These companies used huge dredges to continue mining for gold that could not be easily extracted by prospectors with picks and shovels.

Not all the stampeders left. Some stayed and found work with the mining companies. Others moved out into the bush and lived by trapping, hunting and prospecting. Still others moved to Whitehorse or Carcross. The White Pass and Yukon Railway provided work for some, as did the sternwheelers.

Many of the captains and pilots who worked on the sternwheelers lived in the Yukon only during the summer. They spent the winters with their families in Vancouver or Victoria. The people who supplied wood for the sternwheelers' steam engines often lived along the river year-round. Many of the woodcutters were Native people whose economy also included more traditional activities such as hunting and fishing.

Yukoners and the First World War

When the First World War broke out in August 1914, Yukoners responded with enthusiasm to Canada's call for volunteers. By the end of the year several hundred young men had signed up, and before the war was over an amazing total of 2327 Yukoners — well over one-quarter of the territory's population — had volunteered.

Most went "outside" to enlist, but a couple of prominent residents organized Yukon detachments. On October 10, 1914, a 54-man machine gun unit known as "Boyle's Battery" sailed from Dawson as bands played and crowds cheered. Organized by gold tycoon Joseph Whiteside Boyle, the unit was later broken up, but its members served bravely, collecting a remarkable number of military decorations. Boyle himself, considered too old for active service, managed to get overseas anyway and went on to an

Joe Boyle's Yukon Machine Gun detachment

extraordinary freelance military and diplomatic career. In 1916, Commissioner George Black resigned his post and organized the 17th Yukon Machine Gun Company, which he led to England.

The departure of so many of the territory's young men had a depressing effect on the Yukon's already ailing economy. In 1918, the dwindling population suffered another blow. Canadian Pacific steamships sailed regularly between Skagway and Vancouver. During the summer, they carried tourists. In the fall, they carried out hundreds of Yukon and Alaska workers who were leaving for the winter or for good. The *Princess Sophia,* the last ship to leave that year, had over 300 people on board. On October 25, the ship ran aground on a reef in a blinding blizzard. Small boats from Skagway and Juneau arrived to rescue the passengers, but they were unable to get close to the ship because the winds were so strong. The *Sophia* was still upright the next day, and the little boats again came close to take the passengers off. Again high winds forced them away. Later that day, the *Sophia* sank with 343 passengers and crew. One hundred and twenty-five Dawsonites drowned. Nearly every family in Dawson had a relative or a friend on the *Princess Sophia*.

The 1920s and 1930s

By 1921 the population of the Yukon had dropped to 4157. Dawson and Whitehorse still had hotels and schools, shops and hospitals, but not nearly as many people as before.

The introduction of air transport was one of the few bright spots on the Yukon economic horizon in the 1920s. In 1926, the Yukon Airways and Exploration Company was formed, and a year later the *Queen of the Yukon* became the first commercial "airship." The plane was the sister ship to the famous *Spirit of St. Louis,* in which Charles Lindbergh made the first solo, non-stop flight across the Atlantic.

In the 1930s, the rivers and lakes of the Yukon became landing places for planes belonging to many small companies. In summer the planes were equipped with floats, in winter with skis. It took a lot of

Disembarking from a float plane at Fortymile in July 1938

courage and resourcefulness to fly these early airplanes in the North. Pilots often had to repair their planes themselves. With few instruments and few maps, they had to cope with unmarked terrain and the worst kind of weather. In spite of the difficulties, airplanes soon became a vital form of transportation in the Yukon. The first regular airline service to Edmonton began in 1937. Grant McConachie's United Air Transport Company used the Edmonton–Fort St. John–Whitehorse route. The trip took 15 hours. Later, regular service was offered between Whitehorse and Vancouver. United Air changed its name to Yukon Southern Air and operated until 1942, when it was sold to Canadian Pacific Airlines (CPA). CPA continued to offer daily flights to Vancouver, and is now, under its new name Canadian Airlines International, the only major carrier flying into Whitehorse.

    The Yukon continued to depend primarily on mining in the 1920s and 1930s. In 1934 the United States government raised the set price of gold from $20.67 to $35.00 an ounce. This almost immediately drew another wave of gold-seekers. The world was in the grip of the Great Depression, and the lure of gold was again irresistible. Small deposits that had not been worth mining at the old price now suddenly became attractive. The numbers of people who came to mine were not as great as they were in 1897 and 1898, however.

The Second World War and the Alaska Highway

The Second World War had a major effect on the Yukon. It may seem strange that the tiny territory in northwestern Canada would be strongly affected by a war that began far away in Europe. As the war spread into Asia and the Pacific, however, the United States began to fear a Japanese invasion of Alaska. The first part of the American defence plan called for a series of airfields connecting Alaska with the rest of the United States. The second part called for a road connecting these airfields, so that supplies could be carried by land.

The idea of a road connecting Alaska and the Yukon with points farther south was not new. It had been discussed since 1928, when the International Highway Association was established in Fairbanks, Alaska. British Columbia had supported the idea of such a road because it would make mining and logging in the northwest part of the province easier. A group of business people in the United States had also supported the idea, and several proposed routes had been surveyed.

Even though most of the highway would run through Canada, the Canadian government was unwilling to undertake the expense of building it. The federal government did, however, agree to allow the American army to build it, as long as the Canadian portion was turned over to the Canadian government after the war. Military and civilian road builders started construction in February 1942. The road began in Dawson Creek, British Columbia, and snaked northwestward over the Yukon border to Whitehorse. It continued through the Yukon and over the Alaska border to the town of Delta Junction. The Richardson Highway connected Delta Junction to Fairbanks, Alaska. The whole highway was 2436 kilometres (1514 miles) long.

Whitehorse became the headquarters for much of the Alaska Highway construction. The White Pass and Yukon Railway made it easy to bring in vast quantities of equipment and mountains of supplies. Construction northward was started at Dawson Creek. From Whitehorse, construction crews worked both southward and northward. Another crew worked south from Delta Junction, Alaska. Today, the name of Contact Creek, just south of Watson Lake, Yukon, recalls the meeting of the two crews. Soldier's Summit on Kluane Lake marks the spot where the highway was officially opened in November 1942.

During the construction of the Alaska Highway, Whitehorse's population rose from approximately 500 to nearly 30 000. About 11 000 American soldiers, as well as some 16 000 American and Canadian civilians, worked on the road. The army built construction tent camps and garages, barracks, offices and warehouses, airstrips and roads, a pipeline and an oil refinery. The workers used everything from snowshoes and rubber boots to diesel engines, horses, dogs, rafts and airplanes to survey and build the highway. Many used nothing more complicated than a pick and shovel. One soldier wrote that it was like "mucking around in rivers of mud."

The United States Army leased the White Pass and Yukon Railway and operated the trains. The railway had never been so busy. New engines and cars were brought in to handle the thousands of tonnes of construction equipment and supplies coming into Whitehorse.

The Alaska Highway has been straightened considerably since it was first built. At the beginning, it was full of twists and turns because the surveyors had to lay down a route that was on solid ground. In many places, what appeared to be solid turned out not to be so solid after all.

Northern road builders have a big problem, which the Alaska Highway workers soon discovered: permafrost. When the brush and moss are cleared from the surface, the frozen ground begins to thaw. As a result, the road soon starts to sink. Despite all the difficulties, the initial construction took only eight months and twelve days. The first road was not really a highway at all, however. In some places it was less than a metre (three feet) or so wide, and some of the bridges washed out regularly. Only military and other authorized vehicles were permitted to use it.

The highway was maintained by the United States Army until April 1946, when the Canadian parts of it were turned over to the Canadian Army. Canadian engineers worked for years to improve some 1700 kilometres (1000 miles) of the gravel road. They lowered hills and widened curves. Even so, sections of the road were often closed, and the public was still not allowed to use it without special permits. There were few services on the highway, and travellers

Above: **Building the Alaska Highway, 1942.** *Left:* **This photo of the highway today gives a good idea of the difficulties presented by the terrain through which the road had to pass.**

had to carry several spare tires and whatever extra gas they needed to reach their destination.

In April 1964, the Canadian part of the Alaska Highway became the responsibility of the federal Department of Public Works. Today the Yukon government is responsible for maintenance of the territory's sections. Much of the highway is now covered with a coating called chipseal, which looks like pavement and keeps dust and small rocks to a minimum. Services are now available along the way, but travel on the highway is still not easy, particularly in winter.

Whitehorse and Yukon People Today

Whitehorse grew in the years following the building of the Alaska Highway. The federal and territorial governments expanded. Government workers wanted nice houses and nice neighbourhoods to live in. Today much of the city looks like small cities in other parts of Canada. There are malls, stores and office buildings. The streets are well lit, and there are traffic lights at busy intersections. Familiar fast-food restaurants have opened. There are three radio stations. A local cable company brings in TV stations from as far away as Edmonton, Hamilton and New York. There are two movie theatres, a college and an arts centre. There are separate and public schools, hockey arenas, cross-country and downhill ski facilities, and clubs for almost every sport and hobby.

Transportation has improved between Whitehorse and other communities. There are daily flights to Vancouver and communities in the Yukon, the Northwest Territories and Alaska. Public transit, other than taxis, is a fairly recent introduction. In 1976 a group of women started the Whitehorse Mini-bus Society. Today it is the Whitehorse Transit System. Whitehorse Transit now owns a fleet of ten buses operating on seven routes throughout the city. A Handi-bus serves disabled and elderly passengers who have difficulty using the regular buses. The service operates daily except Sunday.

The population of the Yukon today is about the same as it was during the gold rush. It reached 31 873 in 1992. (In 1993 it shrank a bit because several mines closed.) The Yukon's population is a little less than 0.1 percent of Canada's entire population. This means that only 9 out of every 10 000 Canadians live in the Yukon.

More than 65 percent of Yukoners (23 474) live in Whitehorse. The area within the city boundaries is four times the size of Metropolitan Toronto. Dawson City and Watson Lake are the next largest communities in terms of population, with 1999 and 1845 people, respectively. Most other Yukon communities, such as Mayo, Teslin and Old Crow, are much smaller. Some of the population lives in scattered subdivisions along the highways or in isolated places in the bush and along the rivers.

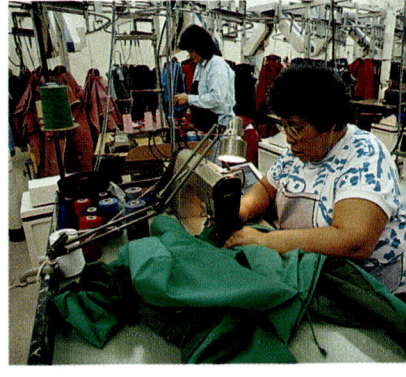

Today, about two-thirds of Yukoners live, work and play in Whitehorse, a thoroughly modern city much like those of comparable size in southern Canada — but with a few unique touches of its very own, including log "skyscrapers" and unbeatable scenery.

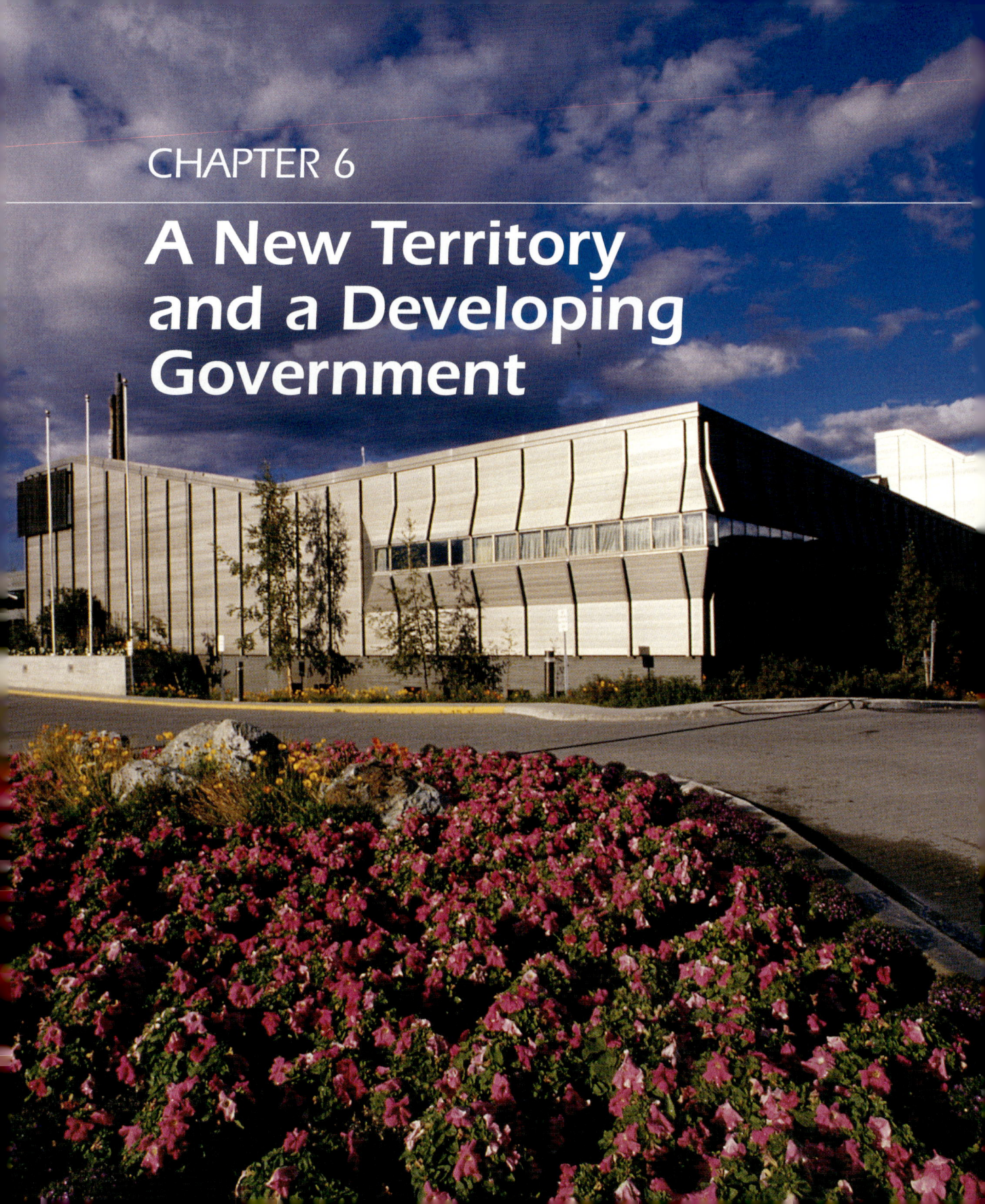

CHAPTER 6
A New Territory and a Developing Government

On June 13, 1898, the Yukon Act made the Yukon District a separate territory of Canada. The federal government had several reasons for passing this act. Not least important was that it needed to make back some of the money it was paying for police and other government services. The easiest way was to collect taxes on all alcohol sold in the Yukon. At the time, the Yukon was a district of the North-West Territories. All tax money, except gold royalties and customs duties, went to the territorial government in Regina, not to Ottawa.

Dawson City was named the capital of the new territory. Major James Walsh of the North West Mounted Police was appointed the first commissioner. He arrived in Dawson in early 1898 but resigned almost immediately and was replaced by William Ogilvie. With a six-member Legislative Council, the commissioner was responsible for public health, education, local administration, roads and other services. (Two more council members were added in 1899.)

By 1902 the Klondike Gold Rush was more or less over. Instead of being mined by prospectors with limited equipment, the creeks were being mined by giant dredges operated by large corporations. Royalties on gold production fattened the federal coffers and, in response, the territory was granted its own member of Parliament (MP). James H. Ross, who had been the Yukon's commissioner, became its first MP. As well, membership in the territorial council grew to 11. Five members were elected and six were appointed.

In 1908 provision was made for a wholly elected council of ten, with elections to be held every three years. This form of local

The Yukon Legislative and Administrative Building

A group photograph of the first wholly elected Territorial Council (10 members plus the Clerk of the Council) taken on the steps of the Administration Building in Dawson, 1909

government continued until 1919. Then, as a result of recession and the Yukon's diminished population of only about 4000, the council was reduced to three members. In following years, the number of council members seesawed with the population and the economic fortunes of the Yukon.

After the Second World War, Whitehorse, with road, air, rail and marine links to the South, became the territory's main communication and business centre. Dawson, northeast of Whitehorse, with a rough road, expensive air service and antiquated riverboats, became increasingly isolated.

In 1953 the capital of the Yukon was moved from Dawson to Whitehorse. Dawsonites, as might be expected, were bitterly opposed to the change. Nevertheless, the government offices moved, as did many businesses.

Responsible Government

Responsible government arrived in the Yukon in 1970, more or less. An executive committee of the Yukon territorial government was

The Yukon Legislature Chamber. The large tapestry in the background required 1400 hours of work and more than 90 kg (200 lbs.) of wool to complete. Entitled *Fireweed* by artist Joanna Staniszkis, it is an abstraction of the Yukon's floral emblem.

formed. It included members of the elected assembly (the former council). For the first time, they took charge of the day-to-day affairs of government. The assembly members were responsible for advising the commissioner in the administration of the territory's affairs. The commissioner, an appointed official, did not have to act on their advice, however.

In 1979 the federally appointed commissioner was removed from the executive committee, and it became a wholly elected executive council, or cabinet. The commissioner was then bound to accept its advice on all matters relating to the territory's areas of jurisdiction. The Executive Council currently has six members.

With these changes, the office of the commissioner who, under the Yukon Act, was officially the head of government, lost much of its power. Ione Christensen, commissioner at the time, announced that her position had become no better than that of a figurehead. She resigned. Today, the commissioner performs duties comparable to those of a lieutenant-governor in one of Canada's provinces. The commissioner reports to the federal minister of Indian Affairs and Northern Development.

The Yukon has one MP in the House of Commons. "Yukon Erik," Conservative Erik Nielson, was the Yukon's MP for 30 years, from 1957 to 1987. During that time he served as deputy prime minister and president of the Privy Council. He was a strong proponent of Native rights and aboriginal title in the Yukon. When Nielson left politics in 1987, Audrey McLaughlin of the New Democratic Party (NDP) won the by-election held to replace him. She was re-elected in 1988 and 1993, and in 1989 became the leader of the federal NDP. The Yukon has one representative in the Canadian Senate.

Territorial Government Today

Currently the Legislative Assembly consists of 17 members who hold terms not exceeding four years. In the election of 1996, the New Democratic Party won eleven seats and formed the government headed by Piers McDonald. The Yukon party and the Yukon Liberal party each won three seats. In a bizarre twist, a tie between the NDP and the Yukon party in one riding was still tied after a recount, resulting in the winner's name — the NDP candidate — being drawn out of a hat.

There are 12 departments in the Yukon government, as well as a Women's Directorate and four Crown corporations, each taking

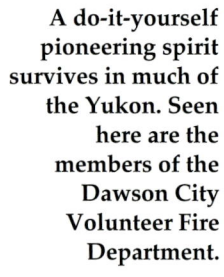

A do-it-yourself pioneering spirit survives in much of the Yukon. Seen here are the members of the Dawson City Volunteer Fire Department.

direction from a cabinet minister. Government departments and agencies are responsible for a wide range of services. These include education, health, economic development, municipal affairs, social services, transportation, housing, tourism, justice, renewable resources and finance. Forestry is in the process of becoming the responsibility of the territorial government.

Over the last decade or so, the federal government has transferred responsibility for the Northern Canada Power Commission, freshwater fisheries, mine safety, inter-territorial roads and the Alaska Highway to the territorial government. Negotiations are underway for the transfer of oil and gas management.

The federal Department of Indian Affairs and Northern Development is jointly responsible with the Yukon government for management of renewable and non-renewable resources on Crown lands.

Education

Yukon schooling follows the British Columbia curriculum, with added content on Yukon heritage. Approximately 6000 public school students attend the territory's 29 public schools, taught by 433 teachers. Classes go from kindergarten through grade 12. Students going on to higher education "outside" are eligible for financial help from the Yukon government.

Yukon College, opened in Whitehorse in 1983, offers a wide range of programs including trades, business and university transfer courses. It has nearly 3500 full- and part-time students. Community learning centres, also called "community campuses," provide some of the programs and courses available at Yukon College to people living elsewhere. A four-year Native education program is offered through the Yukon Native Language Centre, which has a mandate to preserve the languages of the First Nations.

L'Ecole Emilie Tremblay, named after the Québécois owner of a historic Dawson dress store, provides schooling in French for

The Yukon College campus in Whitehorse

French-speaking and French-immersion students. It was established in 1984 and expanded to grade 10 in 1991. French immersion was first introduced in Whitehorse for kindergarten and primary grade children in 1981. It has since been expanded through grade 12.

Health Services

Pioneers settling in the West in the late 1800s were usually isolated from medical help. Concern for the physical well-being of these people was a major reason why the Victorian Order of Nurses (VON) was formed in 1897. A year later, four VON nurses accompanied the Yukon Field Force to Dawson City. The group travelled by rail to Vancouver, then by boat up the British Columbia coast to Wrangell. From there the trail was extremely rough, but the main medical problems the nurses faced on the trip were tending to mosquito bites and blisters. Much worse awaited them in Dawson, where a typhoid epidemic was raging and the Good Samaritan Hospital consisted of two log cabins and a tent.

Left: **One of the two log cabins that constituted the territory's first hospital.**
Right: **VON nurses en route to the Yukon in 1898 (with them, second from right, is Toronto *Globe* reporter Faith Fenton)**

Today, there are two hospitals in the Yukon. They are at Whitehorse and Watson Lake. Besides its hospital, Whitehorse also has a number of private medical clinics. Smaller communities have nursing stations or health stations. Altogether, the territory was served in 1996 by 43 doctors and 26 dentists.

Medical and dental specialists from "outside" hold clinics in Whitehorse on a regular basis. Along with local doctors from Whitehorse, they also visit other communities if necessary. When Yukon residents need special health care not available locally, the government pays for their transportation, drugs, clinic fees and lodging outside the Yukon as required. Medevac allows emergency medical cases to be flown from smaller communities to Whitehorse, or from Whitehorse to Vancouver or Edmonton for treatment.

Justice

The new territorial courthouse in Whitehorse is named for Andrew A. Philipsen, a highly respected territorial minister of justice. Appointed in July 1984, Philipsen, a trucker by trade, was unfortunately killed in an accident on the Dempster Highway in May 1985.

The courts and the administration branch are responsible for justice throughout the Yukon. Whitehorse, Watson Lake and

Dawson City have permanent courtrooms. Court circuits, with local judges and lawyers, regularly visit other communities. Most Yukon communities have resident justices of the peace who deal with minor problems.

In 1960 a special Court of Appeal for the Yukon was established. This consists of the chief justice of British Columbia, the justices of appeal for British Columbia and the judge of the Territorial Court of the Northwest Territories. This special Yukon appeal court has all the powers of the provincial courts of appeal. Judges of the territorial courts of the Northwest Territories and the Yukon may act as judges for both territories.

Court services, a coroner's office and a sheriff's office, a law library, legal aid and probation services are based in Whitehorse. However, they are also available for use by other communities.

The Whitehorse Correctional Institute is the territory's only jail for adults. (There is also a small facility for young offenders.) Offenders serving sentences of more than two years are sent south

The impressive new Law Courts building, Whitehorse

to federal prisons. Most Whitehorse inmates take part in mobile work camps. These provide on-the-job training while prisoners do work that benefits the community. Such work includes clearing roads, building playgrounds and upgrading ski trails.

In recent years, the Yukon government has involved First Nations communities in the sentencing of Native offenders, drawing on traditional Native justice and the experience of elders. The self-government provisions of the First Nations land claims will lead to further changes in this area.

Kathleen Lake, Kluane National Park. *Inset:* **North-West Patrol Welcome Officer. In Whitehorse, students hired by Tourism Yukon and dressed in NWMP uniforms provide visitor information.**

CHAPTER 7
An Economic Portrait

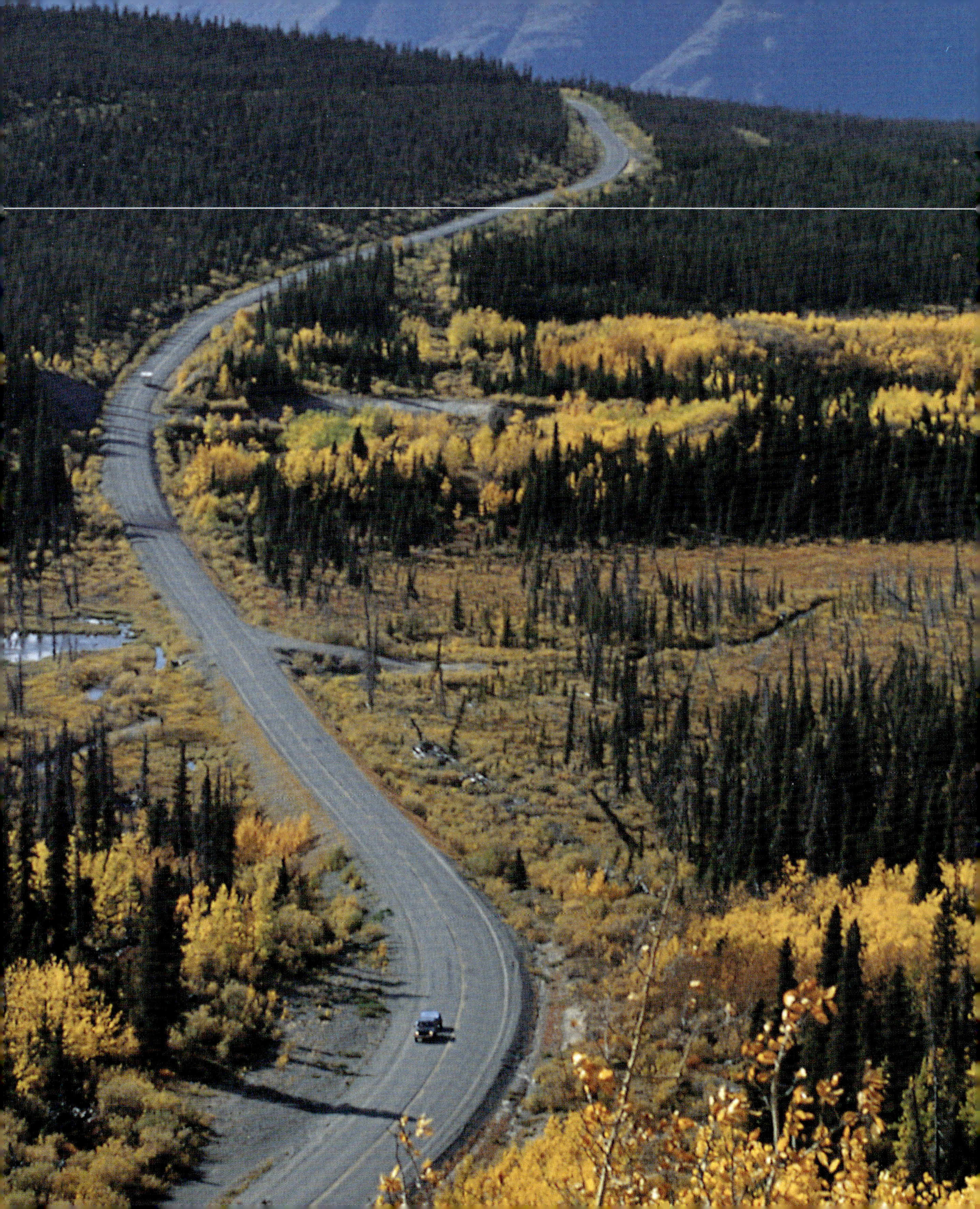

Because of the Yukon's relative remoteness and small population, the territorial economy is heavily subsidized by annual transfer payments from the federal government. Currently these payments total almost half a billion dollars a year. They make up about two-thirds of the territorial budget. Without this subsidy, the Yukon could not exist in its present form.

Mining

Ever since gold was discovered in the Klondike a century ago, mining in one form or another has been the backbone of the territory's non-government economy.

The mining industry has come a long way since prospectors worked with picks and shovels to dig gold from the ground. After the Second World War, minerals such as copper, asbestos, lead, zinc and silver drew a new breed of miners into the Yukon. They flew or drove in, using fixed-wing aircraft, helicopters and four-wheel drive trucks. Their mining camps were an economic boost for the territory. Sales of oil, gas, groceries and equipment, buildings and other necessities benefited Yukon merchants and communities.

In 1995 gold mining accounted for $78 million, or just under 50 percent of the territory's total mineral production: $159 million. Lead, silver and zinc are the other important minerals.

The territory formerly had an asbestos mine at Clinton Creek, northwest of Dawson City. It had a copper mine at Whitehorse and a silver mine at Keno, north of Mayo. The silver at Keno Hill was the

Overleaf: **The Alaska Highway is the Yukon's main link with southern Canada and Alaska.**

Far left: **Gold mining is once again important to the Yukon's economy.** *Left:* **Track drill being used for exploration in the Elsa area**

first major mineral deposit found in the Yukon since the Klondike Gold Rush of the 1890s. Unlike the boom and bust of those days, however, this mining venture provided steady employment for decades. It remained in operation until 1989. In 1996, it was reopened and is expected to be back in production in early 1997. Several other big mines closed in the 1980s, either because the ore was mined out or because world metal prices were so low that it was not worthwhile to continue mining the deposit.

The Yukon's largest mine is a lead-zinc mine at Faro, 356 kilometres (221 miles) northeast of Whitehorse. Working a deposit discovered in the early 1960s, the mine changed the territory. New roads were built, and helicopters became commonplace. Small aircraft companies prospered, as did expediting companies that arranged to get supplies to isolated mining camps. The mining company built a new town, Faro, to provide a base for people working at the mine. The town was nearly completed in 1969 when it burned in a forest fire. It was quickly rebuilt.

Although little mining exploration or mine development had taken place since the beginning of 1990, a new mining boom starting in 1995 has doubled the number of people working in mining and exploration to approximately 2000.

A Vancouver company has bought Casino, a copper-gold-molybdenum property northwest of Carmacks. This may be a

Faro (*clockwise from top*) — the "instant town" that sprang up in 1970; the Anvil Range Mining Company open pit lead-zinc mine; technicians in the mine assay lab testing samples of lead-zinc concentrate

large deposit. It could become an important mine, employing many Yukoners during its two-year construction period and also after it begins to operate. Two potentially large new gold mines are going into production, and several large mining companies are doing extensive exploration in the territory, particularly in the Ross River area.

Conventional high-grade, small-tonnage mining (rich small deposits) is making a comeback while hard rock gold operations, low-grade, high-tonnage mining (poorer large deposits), are breaking new ground. These new operations are causing two of the larger companies to predict production of $900 million in gold over the next ten years.

Clockwise from top: **Cruising historic Miles Canyon on the gold-rush trail to the Klondike; backpackers disembark from the Yukon River Ferry at Dawson City; plane bringing climbers into the Mt. Logan region**

Tourism

The Yukon's history, its wilderness and its highways attract travellers from all over the world. Tourism is the territory's second largest industry. It brings to the territorial economy as much as $100 million annually.

Today's visitors travel to the Yukon by air or by road. Elaborate motor homes are a common sight along Yukon highways in summer. Commercial bus tours, wilderness adventure tours, canoe tripping and river rafting also attract visitors. According to Yukon government figures, approximately 266 000 tourists visited the territory in 1995, spending about $60 million that year. Tourism employs about 3500 people, almost a quarter of the territory's non-government workforce.

Government

Federal, territorial and municipal governments provide Yukoners with more than 4500 jobs. Government is the largest employer in the Yukon, employing about one-third of the territorial workforce. Government employees work in a wide range of jobs. For example, they are clerks, office managers, secretaries, mapmakers, computer programmers and scientists.

Communication and Transportation

There was a telegraph line from Dawson to Skagway during the gold rush. But the Yukon had no effective communications network with southern Canada until 1899, when construction of the Yukon Telegraph Line began. It linked Dawson City to Quesnel, British Columbia, where it hooked up to existing telegraph systems. Completed in 1901, the line was used for several decades. The old telegraph poles have now vanished, but wire and insulators are still found along the old trail. Today NorthwesTel, owned by Bell Canada, provides telecommunications services to the territory.

Yukoners in remote areas often use fixed or mobile radiotelephones. Many of these operate on a regular "sched" (schedule). (A radio sched is a set time once or twice each day when people wait to receive or send messages.) For some, this is their only contact with other people. If they miss more than one of their regular radio times, it alerts others that there may be a problem.

Three radio stations broadcast out of Whitehorse. The Canadian Broadcasting Corporation's CFWH sends programs by microwave to other communities, including Dawson City, Mayo, Faro, Carmacks, Carcross, Watson Lake and Old Crow. CKRW is a privately owned and operated station. CHON-FM, owned and operated by the Yukon Northern Native Broadcasting Society, is transmitted by satellite to 12 Yukon communities. A community radio society also operates in Dawson.

Clockwise from top left: Float plane at Carcross; the Whitehorse Rapids Dam not only generates power, it also provides facilities for viewing the longest migration of Chinook salmon in the world; truck driver at Eagle Plains on the Dempster Highway

    WHTV cable television in Whitehorse carries Canadian and American networks, FM stereo, Pay-TV channels and the Knowledge Network. CBC-TV is available via satellite and relay stations in all Yukon communities.

    Whitehorse has two main newspapers: the daily *Whitehorse Star* and the twice-weekly *Yukon News*. *Dannzha* (formerly the *Yukon Indian News*) and a French-language newspaper come out on a less-regular basis. Other local publications include the monthly *Northern Journal*, the bimonthly *Yukon Reader* and the biannual *Northern Review*, a journal of Yukon College. Dawson, Mayo, Faro, Watson Lake and Haines Junction publish regular news sheets and papers.

    Trucking is an important industry in the Yukon, since most supplies come into the territory by road. As well, trucks move ore from mine sites. The Whitehorse to Skagway section of the Klondike Highway, completed in 1981, was a major factor in the decline of the White Pass and Yukon Railway. Driving an ore truck directly from a mine to the ships at Skagway was less expensive than loading the ore onto a train at Whitehorse and unloading it again at Skagway. The little railway that had played such an important part in the Yukon's history shut down in 1982. Today the White Pass operates as a tourist attraction. Visitors and cruise ship passengers can take a round-trip train to the White Pass summit. Two trains a day go on to the Canadian customs post at Fraser and to Bennett Lake. Transportation and communication today employ about 3000 Yukoners.

Service and Construction Industries

More than 4000 people are employed in service industries. Yukoners work in department stores, service stations, hotels, restaurants, sporting goods stores, music stores, bookstores, gift shops and specialty stores. They also operate computer centres, appliance and engine repair outlets and a variety of other businesses.

More than 568 building permits, valued at over $61 million, were issued in 1995 for residential, industrial, institutional and commercial buildings. The construction industry employs approximately 1000 people.

Furs, Forests, Farming, Fishing and Hunting

The fur trade is the Yukon's oldest industry. It was back in 1842 that the Hudson's Bay Company first began exploring the territory to expand its fur trading empire.

Today, trapping provides a livelihood for about 800 Yukoners. It is an uncertain occupation, since fur prices fluctuate with the demand from season to season. The worldwide demand for fur coats and other fur clothing has dwindled in recent years, and so have prices of pelts. Fourteen types of animals are trapped for their furs in the territory. These include beavers, martens, lynxes, foxes and minks.

Fur production in 1995 was worth $295 000, down drastically from 1988's $1.35 million. Fox pelts sold for $33 in 1988, but brought only $25 in 1995.

Forestry is not an important industry in the Yukon. A Yukon tree takes at least 50 years to reach maturity — if it escapes a forest fire.

Top: Haying in the Dawson area. *Bottom:* On an island in the Yukon River, Grant and Karen Dowdell have developed a successful market garden operation. Their fresh vegetables, which Grant delivers in his home-made boat, are much appreciated in nearby Dawson.

Fires, started mainly by lightning strikes, destroy millions of hectares of trees every year. The fires do, however, allow new growth, which provides food for wildlife.

Timber operators work on a seasonal basis, mostly at three small mills near Watson Lake in southeastern Yukon. Some of the lumber goes to Alaska but most is used locally. A recent venture by the Kaska Dene Nation is harvesting raw logs for export to Japan. Several small sawmills operate near Whitehorse. Fewer than 30 people work in the industry, and they work on a part-time basis.

Areas that are good for farming in the Yukon are limited because of poor soil, low rainfall and the problem of permafrost. On the other hand, the long hours of sunlight help plants grow quickly. While agriculture is not an important part of the territory's overall economy, there are a number of successful farming operations. Near Dawson, for example, where occasional flooding from the rivers has enriched the soil, vegetables and field crops such as hay grow well. One family runs a thriving market garden on an island in the Yukon River above Dawson. The produce is in great demand locally.

The Whitehorse area has a growing number of small, family-run commercial farms. Vegetables, ornamental plants, seeds, turf, pigs, chickens, rabbits, goats, sheep, cattle, fish and reindeer are the chief products.

Another well-known operation is the Bradley brothers' farm on the lower Pelly River. For many years, the Bradleys have successfully raised a variety of crops, as well as cattle. However, there are drawbacks to raising animals in the Yukon. All meat animals must be shipped out for processing because the territory does not have it's own licensed facilities.

As you might expect, fishing is more important to the Yukon economy than farming. Chinook and chum salmon caught in the rivers near Dawson are processed locally and sold in Germany, Japan and other countries. Fresh salmon is sold locally in season, and dried or smoked salmon is popular as well. Trout are also plentiful and are sold commercially. Just outside Whitehorse, Polar Sea Fisheries raises arctic char, a northern delicacy sold to restaurants worldwide.

It is, however, mostly sport fishing that brings in dollars. Anglers from all over the world come to fish in the territory's fast clear streams and deep cold lakes. Only a few lakes near Whitehorse are fished regularly and, even in these waters, anglers are rarely disappointed. Sport fishing contributes approximately $5 million annually to the Yukon economy.

The dollar value of hunting in the Yukon is difficult to determine.

Yukon First Nations have special hunting rights and do not require licences. Non-resident big-game hunting for grizzly and black bears, moose, sheep and caribou contributes about $1 million annually to the territorial economy. This includes its spinoffs, such as guiding and outfitting services provided to the hunters. Another $450 000 annually is added by non-Native resident hunters.

Left: **Traditional Native fish traps are still used in some parts of the Yukon.** *Below right:* **A salmon to be proud of.** *Below left:* **While a small, but growing, commercial fishing industry exists, it is as a sport that fishing contributes most to the Yukon economy.**

CHAPTER 8
Arts and Recreation

Most Yukoners live in the territory by choice, not because they were born there. As people move north, they bring along their energy, ideas, talent and sense of adventure. This contributes to the Yukon's broad cultural base.

The Yukon's remoteness from the rest of Canada provides an uncritical environment that encourages people to experiment. From painting to playwriting, storytelling to dog sledding, all things seem possible. The arts are strongly represented, and so are sports.

Performing Arts

Whitehorse is the hub for non-Native cultural activities in the Yukon. Many events are held at the new Yukon Arts Centre, beside the Yukon College complex. Year-round, theatre groups, singers, dancers, musicians, storytellers and concert groups perform here and elsewhere in the city. These entertainers also travel to other communities in the territory, usually performing in local schools.

For a week in February, Whitehorse is transformed by the Yukon Sourdough Rendezvous. Started by the American military during the Second World War, this festival celebrates the beginning of the end of winter. Generally the whole town turns out to take part, and many residents dress up in turn-of-the-century costumes. Banks, shops and restaurants are decorated with a gold rush theme. There are sled-dog races, beard-growing contests, dances, sports events, concerts and fiddle contests. The Frostbite Music Festival is also

Boats at Rest by Ted Harrison

Reliving gold rush days with *(left to right)* **cast members Dawson's** *Gaslight Follies,* **Whitehorse's** *Frantic Follies* **and a participant in the Yukon Sourdough Rendezvous flour-packing contest**

part of the fun. **Workshops** and concerts attract people from all over the Yukon, as well as from "outside."

The Guild Hall in Porter Creek, a Whitehorse suburb, hosts several plays each winter. Musical events, art and photography shows and public lectures are also held there.

In summer the longest-running production is the Frantic Follies Vaudeville Show. For 25 summers, this rowdy, cheerful event has presented dances, skits and songs on the Klondike theme. Another colourful, lively show is the Canteen Show, a slapstick comedy about the building of the Alaska Highway. Public presentations of poems by Robert Service, as well as music hall songs and skits, are always popular.

Native and non-Native storytellers from all over northern Canada keep audiences spellbound with their tales of fact, fantasy and legend at the Yukon International Storytelling Festival. This is held each July in Whitehorse. Native storytellers — including P.J. Johnson, Louise Profeit-LeBlanc and the late Angela Sidney — are among those who have helped preserve and promote Native culture in the territory.

The children's story tent at the Yukon International Storytelling Festival. This festival has grown enormously in popularity since its rather humble beginnings less than a decade ago. It now attracts storytellers from as far away as Finland and northern Japan, and thousands of eager listeners.

The highlight of the Yukon social scene each summer is the formal Commissioner's Ball held at the Palace Grand Theatre in Dawson. Originally built in 1899 by gold rush entrepreneur Arizona Charlie Meadows and rebuilt by the federal government in 1962, the Palace Grand is also home to the Gaslight Follies.

One of the territory's most popular cultural events is the Dawson City Music Festival. Each July it brings musicians from all over the continent to make music under the midnight sun.

Discovery Days in Dawson have been celebrated ever since gold was discovered in the Klondike. They are always held on the weekend closest to August 17, and the events haven't changed much since 1900. Dawson's population doubles for the weekend as everyone takes part in the fun. It includes a parade, dances, raft and canoe races and fruit and flower shows.

Wearable and Visual Arts

Yukon First Nations faced a harsh natural environment, which called for a migratory lifestyle. They had no use for the heavy carved items and permanent houses for which their Pacific coast neighbours are known. Instead, much of their creative ability went into their clothing, which is still some of the finest made. Home-

Right: A Native embroiderer at work. *Far right:* A particularly fine pair of beaded moccasins on display at the McBride Museum in Whitehorse

tanned moose hide moccasins, mukluks, mitts and jackets are soft and warm and are beautifully decorated with beads, leather, fur and embroidery. Parkas — double layer coats in warm duffel and waterproof cloth — are decorated with traditional designs and topped with fur-trimmed hoods.

Moosehair tufting, the painstaking art of transforming small clumps of carefully trimmed moosehair into pictures of rose petals or pussy willows, is particularly prized. Small carvings, moose horn jewellery and other First Nations works of art are found in stores in most communities.

Few painters have captured the public's fascination with the North as well as Ted Harrison. A school teacher, Harrison came to the Yukon in 1968. His brilliantly coloured, stylized scenes of the North have made him famous. Harrison is also well known for his children's books; his illustrated poems of Robert Service; a northern alphabet about bears, berries, moose and mukluks; and a book of paintings about Canada.

In 1929, Lilias Farley was a member of the first class to graduate from the Vancouver School of Decorative and Applied Arts. In 1948, she came to see her brother in Whitehorse for what she intended as "a short visit." She ended up staying until her death in 1989. Farley's first love was sculpting. Her marble bust, *Woman,* is in the Yukon Territory Permanent Collection. Though her output was

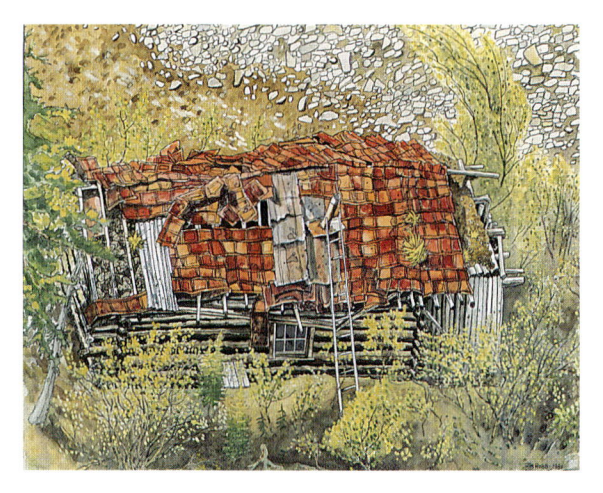

Far left: **Watercolour entitled** *Miller Creek Blacksmith Shop* **by Jim Robb.** *Middle:* **Salmon** *Woman,* **a painted cedar mask, by Tlingit carver Keith Wolfe Smarch.** *Left:* **Woman, by Lilias Farley**

small, her work is famous for its clean, strong lines in wood or stone. Her work may now be found in Vancouver and New York galleries, and in many private collections.

Jim Robb, Chris Caldwell, Bill Barney and Layla Bevan are among other artists whose work is in private collections and public galleries. Other Yukoners who have made a name for themselves in the arts include Tlingit carver Keith Wolfe Smarch and sculptors Alyx Jones and Kate Williams.

Literature

Pierre Berton's books about the Yukon are famous. His mother, Laura Beatrice Berton, also wrote a well-known book. She came to Dawson in 1907 to teach kindergarten. She married in the Yukon, had children and stayed until 1932. Her book, *I Married the Klondike,* is an enthralling story of life in a fading frontier town. Berton often mentions Yukoner Martha Black, who wrote her own memorable book, *My Seventy Years* — later updated to *My Ninety Years.*

Jack London's *The Call of the Wild* and many of his other books and short stories are based on his year in the Klondike during the gold rush. Robert Service, a bank clerk also inspired by the gold rush, wrote books of famous poems about the Yukon including "The Cremation of Sam McGee" and "The Shooting of Dan McGrew."

"There are strange things done in the midnight sun/By the men who moil for gold..." So begins Robert Service's immortal "The Cremation of Sam McGee." Seen here are the cover picture for Ted Harrison's delightful illustrated edition of the poem and Service himself, sitting in front of his Dawson cabin around 1910.

Al Wright experienced a different Yukon before the gold rush, and Lewis Green wrote about gold mining in the creeks after the stampeders had gone. Dick North tells tales of heroes and heroic events. Robert Coutt's *Yukon Places and Names* offers fascinating glimpses of history. Many Yukoners have written about personalities or places, past and present, with affection and understanding. A recent book, *Writing North,* is an anthology by contemporary Yukon writers.

Among Yukon playwrights are Leslie Hamson, Patti Flather and Leonard Linklater.

Local photographers have produced books of pictures that capture, at least in part, what is unique about this beautiful territory.

Sports

A large proportion of the Yukon population is young. Sports, winter and summer, play an important part in people's lives. One in three Yukoners is registered with a recognized sports body. As far back as 1905, the Nuggets, a Dawson City hockey team, travelled 6400 kilometres (4000 miles) to play against Ottawa's Silver Seven in a

Top: **Undaunted by the cold, Whitehorse youngsters take full advantage of the world-class cross-country skiing facilities available virtually at their doorstep.** *Bottom left:* **Getting set for the blanket toss, one of several traditional Native sports featured at the Arctic Winter Games.** *Right:* **Sean Sheardown after winning his cycling gold at the 1989 Canada Games**

two-game series for the Stanley Cup. The Nuggets unfortunately lost both games, 9-2 and an incredible 23-2. However, they did well in an exhibition series.

Whitehorse has some of the most modern sports facilities in the country. Hockey, baseball, curling and cross-country skiing facilities are excellent. The city frequently hosts regional, national and international competitions. Numerous tracked and groomed cross-country trails ramble through the bush and up and down mountains on the outskirts of Whitehorse and several smaller communities. Some trails are lit for night skiing.

Whitehorse has a Triple-A team, the Huskies, in the Pacific Northwest Hockey League. Other teams in the league are Fairbanks, Anchorage and Penticton. Two Whitehorse players have been spotted by talent scouts — Bobby House for the Chicago Black Hawks in 1991 and Jarrett Deuling for the New York Islanders in 1992.

When taking part in southern competitions, northern athletes must travel long distances, often at their own expense. For many athletes, this makes it difficult to participate. The Arctic Winter Games (AWG), started in 1970, offer athletes from the Yukon, Northwest Territories, Alaska, northern Russia and Greenland the opportunity to compete in the North. The games also give athletes experience and valuable training. As well as regular sports, the AWG have traditional Indian and Inuit sports, such as the blanket toss and the ear-pulling contest. The games are rotated between four locations: the Yukon, the Northwest Territories, Alaska and northern Alberta.

In 1987 four Yukoners won silver medals at the Canada Games in Nova Scotia for cross-country skiing and weightlifting. In later games, Sean Sheardown of Whitehorse won in cycling and cross-country skiing, becoming the first athlete ever to win medals in both winter and summer Canada Games. In the 1991 Winter Games in Prince Edward Island, Yukon athletes came home with 17 medals — four gold, ten silver and three bronze.

Dogsled racing ("mushing") is an important sport in the North. The longest dogsled race in the Yukon is the Yukon Quest, 1600 kilometres (1000 miles), between downtown Whitehorse and Fairbanks, Alaska. Started in 1984, the Quest retraces the route used by Yukon pioneers, miners and Mounties, missionaries and mail carriers. The starting point for the Quest alternates each year between Whitehorse and Fairbanks. When it is Whitehorse's turn, large crowds line First Avenue, whatever the temperature. They watch 40 or more mushers in heavy parkas, sleds laden with food and gear, taking off at two-minute intervals down the street and out onto the frozen Yukon River. The Quest is known as the toughest dogsled race in the world. Mushers and their dogs train all year for the gruelling race, pulling wheeled carts or old car chassis in summer. Shorter races are also held in most communities.

In summer, Yukoners and visitors from around the globe enjoy the challenge of mountain climbing, canoeing, kayaking, white-water rafting and river rafting. Mountain biking, especially around Kluane Park and on Grey Mountain in Whitehorse, is becoming popular. People also enjoy horseback riding, swimming and baseball or softball games under the soft evening sun. Whitehorse has two golf courses; Watson Lake and Dawson have one each. Year-round indoor sports include gymnastics, archery, fencing and volleyball. Virtually the whole territory — serene, isolated and unspoiled — is a delight for campers, hikers, hunters and anglers.

Yukoners are blessed with some of the world's most pristine lakes and streams and some of its most beautiful scenery in which to enjoy their choice of outdoor sports.

CHAPTER 9

Touring the Territory

The Yukon has 4480 kilometres (2784 miles) of highways linking the scattered communities spread so thinly across this vast, rugged territory. Their names reflect Yukon history and culture, from the Haines Road #3, to the Robert Campbell #4, Canol #6, Atlin #7, Tagish #8, Top of the World #9, Nahanni Range #10 and Silver Trail #11.

Following is a territorial tour focussing on three of the Yukon's longest highways — The Alaska #1, Klondike #2 and Dempster #5 — and ending with Old Crow, the only Yukon community not served by a road.

The Alaska Highway, #1

The Alaska Highway winds its way through 1000 kilometres (625 miles) of northern British Columbia before reaching its first Yukon community, Watson Lake.

Watson Lake

The area around Watson Lake in the southeast was originally inhabited by Kaska people. The town was named after a British trapper, Frank Watson, who was headed for the Klondike but settled here instead and married a Kaska woman in 1898.

With a population of 1845, Watson Lake is the third-largest Yukon community. It was a major centre during the building of the Alaska

Clockwise from top right: **Cancan dancers at Diamond Tooth Gertie's Gambling Hall, Canada's first legalized gambling casino, in Dawson. The real Gertie got her nickname from the diamond she had wedged between her two front teeth; tourists panning for gold at Claim 33, Bonanza Creek; a favourite exhibit at the MacBride Museum in Whitehorse is the real Sam McGee's cabin; Native children from the Selkirk Indian Band at Pelly Crossing; Our Lady of the Way chapel, Haines Junction**

The *only* roads in the Yukon

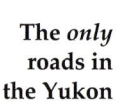

1	Alaska Highway
2	Klondike Highway
3	Haines Road
4	Campbell Highway
5	Dempster Highway
6	Canol Road
7	Atlin Road
8	Tagish Road
9	Top of the World Highway
10	Nahanni Range Road
11	Silver Trail

— Principal Roads (asphalt)
--- Principal Roads (gravel)
··· Secondary Roads

(Map is not to scale)

Highway in 1942. A homesick American soldier put up a sign pointing towards his home in Danville, Illinois. Other people copied the idea and now there are about 20 000 signs in the famous "Signpost Forest." The Alaska Highway Interpretive Centre has an audio-visual show and displays about the construction of the highway.

From Watson Lake the Alaska Highway heads west across the southern Yukon towards Alaska. At kilometre 1160 (mile 725), it crosses the Continental Divide — the boundary between rivers that drain into the Arctic Ocean and those that drain into the Pacific.

Far left: Another sign joins the forest at Watson Lake, the first Yukon community on the Alaska Highway. *Above:* Nisutlin Bay Bridge across Teslin Lake. *Left:* Tlingit drum dancers from Teslin

Teslin

The Nisutlin Bay Bridge across Teslin Lake, at kilometre 1292 (mile 803) is the longest bridge on the highway. It has a span of 575 metres (1886 feet) and leads to the community of Teslin.

Teslin is home to one of the largest First Nations communities in the Yukon, with a population of about 460. Originally the summer home of Interior Tlingit people, the settlement became permanent in 1903 with the founding of a trading post there. The George Johnston Museum has the largest collection of Tlingit artifacts in the territory. There are also rare photographs and dioramas. Native woodworking skills are demonstrated at Teslin Tlingit Woodcrafts, which sells beautifully handcrafted items.

The Alaska Highway continues to Whitehorse, running beside the waters of Marsh Lake.

Whitehorse

Whitehorse, capital of the territory, has more than 23 000 residents — two-thirds of the Yukon's population. It owes its existence to its location at the head of the navigable waters for river boats. Its name comes from the nearby Yukon River Rapids, which, one story has it, early settlers thought resembled the flowing manes of white horses.

Whitehorse lies on the west bank of the Yukon River. Besides the downtown residential area, the city is surrounded by eight subdivisions. Houses along the wide streets range from little wooden ones predating the Alaska Highway to large, modern homes. In the downtown section, modern government buildings sit side by side with older, single-storey structures, including a few log cabins, still in use. The two- and three-storey "log-skyscrapers" two blocks south of Main Street are a major tourist attraction.

For tourists, the city has a variety of attractions, many with a gold rush theme. The S.S. *Klondike*, the largest — and last — of the 250 sternwheelers that steamed along the Yukon River, can be toured. Exhibits at the Old Log Church, built in 1900, focus on the activities of some well-known missionaries. The MacBride Museum has exhibits ranging from prehistory to the present. The Yukon's Permanent Art Collection is displayed in the spacious foyer of the Yukon Territorial Government Building.

Whitehorse. *Right:* Top dog mushers from across North America compete in the annual Yukon Quest race from Whitehorse to Fairbanks, Alaska. *Far right, top:* The Old Log Church Museum houses exhibits showing the history of the territory. *Bottom :* The **S.S.** *Klondike*, designated a National Historic Site, has been restored to reflect the late 1930s.

The Yukon Archives, beside Yukon College, have extensive information on the territory's past, as does the Yukon Transportation Museum beside the airport. From sleds to airplanes, the museum relates the Yukon's transportation history.

A cruise through Miles Canyon, called the Grand Canyon by early miners, gives a glimpse of what the prospectors faced in their rush north. Tamed by a hydroelectric dam in the late 1950s, the waters of the canyon no longer rage between the high basalt walls, although the water still runs swiftly.

A dip in soothing hot springs or cool Long Lake, professional music and plays, talks and slide shows, and fishing and hiking on the edge of the city all contribute to Whitehorse's varied lifestyle. As well, the city has extensive sports facilities, excellent restaurants, shops, malls, theatres and cinemas.

From Whitehorse, the Alaska Highway runs west to Haines Junction, on the edge of Kluane National Park.

Haines Junction

The mountains are seen almost everywhere in this pleasant community of 700 people. The Southern Tutchone name for Haines

Far left: There are 4480 km (2784 mi.) of highways in the Yukon offering fabulous routes for scenic touring. These visitors view the St. Elias Mountain range from a lookout in Kluane National Park. *Left:* Visitors view Kluane glaciers from the air.

Right: Cabin in the ghost town of Silver City. In existence from 1904-1924, it was the site of a trading post and North West Mounted Police barracks on the road from Whitehorse to the Kluane gold fields. *Bottom left:* The Kluane Museum of Natural History at Burwash Landing features Native artifacts and natural dioramas of Yukon wildlife. *Bottom right:* Church at Beaver Creek constructed out of a Quonset hut and built on a platform to avoid shifting caused by permafrost

Junction is Dakwakada, meaning "meat cache." It was not a traditional First Nations settlement, but was a provisioning point en route to the rich salmon runs at Klukshu. Today, Haines Junction is the headquarters of the Champagne–Aishihik First

Nation, which has played a leading role in the settlement of the Yukon land claims.

The community is strongly tourist oriented. Many visitors come to explore Kluane National Park, which was designated as a UNESCO World Heritage Site in 1979. A number of Haines Junction people have jobs related to tourism. For example, some operate helicopter or fixed-wing flights over Mount Logan or the Kaskawulsh and Lowell glaciers. Some act as guides for fishing, hunting, hiking, whitewater rafting or climbing.

Destruction Bay and Burwash Landing are two tiny communities passed along the Alaska Highway before the Canadian section ends at Beaver Creek, kilometre 1934 (mile 1202). Beaver Creek is Canada's westernmost community. Many of its 114 people work for the government in customs or the post office.

The Klondike Highway, #2

The Klondike Highway roughly parallels the route taken by the gold stampeders of 1898. Between Skagway and Carcross, it climbs to the summit of the White Pass at 1004 metres (3290 feet).

Carcross

This was the home of Tagish people, who traded with the coastal Tlingit and eventually adopted their language. Later it became a place for gold stampeders to stop and rest after their long trip up Lake Bennett. The last spike on the White Pass and Yukon Railway was driven at Carcross in 1900.

Picturesque Matthew Watson's General Store and the Caribou Hotel date from the turn of the century. Both are fronted by a wooden boardwalk built beside the wide main street.

Just north of this community of 375 is the "Carcross Desert," an area of ancient sand dunes in constant motion from winds funnelled along Lake Bennett. It is claimed by some to be the smallest desert in the world.

Above: **Emerald Lake alongside the Klondike Highway, north of Carcross. Its brilliant green colour is said to be caused by the copper-bearing rocks on the bottom of the lake.** *Right:* **Carcross cemetery, burialplace of "Skookum Jim" and "Tagish Charlie" who found gold at Bonanza Creek and started the Klondike Gold Rush. Tagish Charlie's headstone reads "Dawson Charlie."**

Carmacks

Carmacks was once a camp along a trade route between the coastal Chilkat Tlingit and the interior Athapaskans. Located at kilometre 357 (mile 222), it got its present name from George Carmack, one of the discoverers of the gold that started the Klondike Gold Rush. It currently has a population of 400.

Five Finger Rapids is just north of Carmacks. An observation deck overlooking the rapids gives an excellent view of these turbulent waters.

From Carmacks most of the Klondike Highway follows the Yukon Valley. But at Minto, it diverges to Pelly Crossing, on the Pelly River. The home of the Selkirk Indian Band, Pelly Crossing has a population of 270.

The Yukon River's tributaries, including the Pelly (above), Teslin, Stewart and Big Salmon, are popular with novice canoeists. While a few rough sections of water can be expected, for the most part these rivers are characterized by fast-flowing, flat water — perfect for the paddler.

Dawson City

Dawson City lies at the junction of the Yukon and Klondike rivers. Dawson was named for Dr. George Dawson, a federal government geologist who explored the area in 1887 and predicted a major gold strike in the area. He was right. By 1898 the former fishing camp had turned into the largest city west of Winnipeg.

Despite its later changes in fortune, Dawson has never lost its romantic glitter as the centre of the Klondike Gold Rush. Tourists come each summer to wander the town's wide streets and wooden boardwalks. Until recently they could conduct business at the Canadian Bank of Commerce where bank clerk and poet Robert Service once worked. Sitting on benches outside Service's little log cabin, surrounded by willows and fireweed, visitors listen while actors bring his poetry to life.

Gold rush and earlier artifacts are on display at the Dawson City Museum. Visitors can pan for gold on the creeks and tour great dredges at their sinuous tailing piles. Many of the area's historic buildings feature guided tours, slide shows or films on Dawson in the gold rush era.

Dawson's streets are laid out in tidy squares. Their brightly painted houses and false-fronted stores and hotels are enhanced by brilliant flower gardens. Huge iron buckets from the gold dredges decorate some gardens as flower containers.

Dawson lies under the shadow of the Midnight Dome. It is a local tradition to drive to the top of the 630-metre (2000-foot) hill on the longest day each year to see the sun at midnight.

Dawson City. *Clockwise from bottom:* **Famous view of the city and the Yukon River from the Midnight Dome; Front Street today — even the new construction has the spirit of gold rush days; antique locomotives from the Klondike Mines Railway in front of the Dawson City Museum, which is housed in the old Territorial Administration building, built in 1901; the old hardware store, a reminder of days gone by**

The Dempster Highway, #5

Completed in 1979, the Dempster Highway starts 40 kilometres (25 miles) east of Dawson and ends in Inuvik, Northwest Territories. The only Canadian road to cross the Arctic Circle, it runs through unspoiled wilderness all the way. To protect the fragile arctic tundra, much of the narrow route is built 10 metres (33 feet) above the ground, on a wall of crushed black rock. The rock provides insulation to stop the underlying permafrost from melting.

In recent years, visitors crossing the Arctic Circle on the Dempster Highway have been delighted to be greeted by an elderly gentleman formally dressed in top hat and tails, sitting in a rocking chair. Self-appointed "Keeper of the Arctic Circle," he began entertaining tourists in his spare time. He became so popular that he was appointed to the "position" full-time during the summer months.

Top of the World Highway, west of Dawson City. Open to summer traffic only, this highway winds through mountains and valleys to the Yukon-Alaska border.

Right: Dempster Highway, named after North West Mounted Police Corporal W.J. Dempster who found the famous lost patrol. The Dempster is the only public highway in North America that crosses the Arctic Circle. *Above:* "Keeper of the Arctic Circle," an imaginary line that encircles the earth about 2623 km (1630 mi.) from the North Pole

Old Crow

The only Yukon community with no road connections is Old Crow. This Native community of 277 is 120 kilometres (72 miles) north of the Arctic Circle. Everything from outside comes into Old Crow by air. There is a small airport, and float planes use the river.

Archaeologists think people may have been living in the Old Crow Flats about 24 000 years ago. If this is true, it is one of the oldest sites of human habitation in North America. Its name comes from the Gwich'in people, who called the area "walking crow" (raven) after a famous chief.

The community's economy centres on hunting, fishing and trapping. Some local people work for government branches and for exploration and scientific parties in the vicinity.

Left: Float planes carry visitors, residents and supplies in and out of Old Crow, the only Yukon community inaccessible by road. This is also true of Ivvavik National Park in the northwest corner of the territory. Here the Firth River *(below)* winds through the British Mountains delighting visitors with views of spectacular wildlife and arctic tundra plains cut into canyons.

For years Old Crow elder Edith Josie's columns, called "Here Are the News," were published regularly in the *Whitehorse Star* and in many southern newspapers. They brought southerners glimpses of a unique northern lifestyle. Josie's columns still appear sometimes in the *Star* and have been published in two books.

Facts at a Glance

General Information

Became a Territory: June 13, 1898

Territorial Capital: Whitehorse

Nickname: Land of the Midnight Sun

Territorial Flag: The Yukon flag is green, white and blue, representing the forests, snow and pristine rivers and lakes. The coat of arms is on the white portion.

Coats of Arms: The wavy blue and white stripes down the centre of the shield represent the Yukon River and its tributaries. The red spire-like forms indicate the mountains, and the gold discs are the mineral resources. The St. George's Cross is a tribute to the British explorers and fur traders. The rondel with the bell-like forms is symbolic of the fur trade. The malamute dog standing on a mound of snow atop the shield symbolizes the important part these dogs played in the Yukon's early history.

Territorial Flower: Fireweed

Territorial Bird: Raven

Territorial Gem: Lazulite

People

Population: 33 000 (July 1996)

Population Density: 0.07 people per km^2 (0.18 per sq. mi.)

Population Distribution: 65% of Yukoners live in the capital and only city, Whitehorse. Dawson and Watson Lake each have about 4% of the population. Faro has 3%. The remaining 24% live in the Yukon's other 13 communities or in isolated areas.

Population Variation:
1901	27 219
1911	8 512
1921	4 157
1931	4 230
1941	4 914
1951	9 096
1961	14 628
1971	18 390
1981	23 153
1991	30 453
1996	33 000

Geography

Borders: The Yukon is bordered on the south by British Columbia and on the west by the state of Alaska. The Beaufort Sea lies to the north, and the Northwest Territories lie to the east.

Total Area: 483 450 km^2 (186 675 sq. mi.)

Highest Point: Mount Logan, in the St. Elias Range. At 5959 metres (19 550 feet), it is the highest mountain in Canada.

Lowest Point: Sea level at the Arctic shore

Principal Rivers: Yukon, Stewart, Pelly, Teslin, Alsek, Donjek, Klondike, Liard, MacMillan, McQuesten, Nisutlin, Peel, Porcupine, Ross, Snake, White and Wind

Lakes: There are many small lakes in the Yukon, but most are in the south because the north and central areas were not glaciated during the last Ice Age. The largest lakes are Aishihik, Bennett, Dezadeash, Frances, Kluane, Kusawa, Laberge, Little Salmon, Marsh, Mayo, Quiet, Tagish and Teslin.

Time Zone: The Yukon has one official time zone: Pacific Standard.

Topography: The Yukon is part of the Canadian Cordillera, a region of hills, mountains and deep valleys. The territory's most outstanding feature is the basin-like Yukon Plateau, a high, rolling upland that has been sculptured into rounded mountains and U-shaped valleys by ice and the Yukon River. The Yukon Plateau covers much of the central and southern Yukon. Slashing northwest across the plateau are the Tintina and Denali faults. Smaller plateaus are the Peel in the north and the Liard in the southeast.

National Parks: Kluane, Ivvavik (formerly Northern Yukon), Vuntut

Territorial Parks: Herschel Island, Coal River

Wildlife Sanctuaries: Kluane, McArthur

Climate: The Yukon has long, cold winters with very short days and long nights. Summers are warm with long, sunny days. Mountainous conditions contribute to strong variations in temperature and precipitation across the territory. Precipitation is generally low, ranging from 230 to 430 mm (9.5 to 17.5 in.). Whitehorse has about 82 frost-free days a year. Mean temperatures recorded at Whitehorse are -19°C (-2°F) in January, and 14°C (57°F) in July.

Nature

Trees: Forest covers 281 030 km^2 (108 514 sq. mi.) of the Yukon, more than 50% of the land area. The few species of trees grow slowly. They include black and white spruce, lodgepole pine, trembling aspen, balsam poplar, birch, tamarack, willow and alder.

Wildflowers: Wildflowers in profusion colour the land as soon as the snow begins to melt. They include Yukon crocuses, wild roses, tundra

Archaeological dig at Herschel Island Territorial Park, once an important whaling harbour

Sled dog at rest

roses, purple vetch, arctic poppies, marsh marigolds, pussy paws, Jacob's ladder, forget-me-nots and orchids. Fireweed, the last of summer flowers, grows profusely in burned areas and along roadsides.

Animals: Large mammals of the Yukon include grizzly and black bear, wolf, coyote, moose, mule deer, caribou, Dall's sheep, mountain goat and cougar. Polar bear, seal and walrus are found along the Arctic shoreline. Smaller mammals include ground squirrel, hoary marmot, red squirrel, hare, porcupine, fox, beaver, wolverine and mink.

Birds: Predatory birds found in the Yukon include the bald eagle, golden eagle, owls, hawks, peregrine and gyrfalcon. Game birds such as geese, swans, loons, and many kinds of ducks nest in the territory. Perching birds include sparrows, swallows, larks, bluebirds, chickadees, jays and ravens.

Fish: The Yukon is famous for its sport fishing. Salmon varieties include chinook, coho and sockeye. Other major species are lake trout, Dolly Varden trout, arctic grayling, arctic char, rainbow trout, northern pike, whitefish and ling cod.

Government

Territorial: The Yukon has a federally appointed commissioner who fulfils duties comparable to those of a provincial lieutenant-governor. The Yukon government leader and 6-member Executive Council assume responsibility for policy and decision making except in areas under the control of the federal government. Executive Council members are also elected members of the Yukon Legislative Assembly. The Assembly has 17 elected members, 7 of whom represent ridings in Whitehorse.

Federal: The Yukon elects one member to the House of Commons and has one federally appointed senator. The federal government still has a strong presence in the territory. The Yukon territorial government is gradually assuming more responsibility, though financing still comes mainly from the federal government.

Education

Education is the responsibility of the Yukon territorial government. The curriculum is based on British Columbia's, with added Yukon heritage content. Elementary and secondary education is available through 12 grades. Approximately 6060 students attend the territory's 29 schools. Native language programs are available through the Yukon Native Language Centre. French immersion is offered for kindergarten to Grade 10, and L'Ecole Emilie Tremblay provides French-language schooling. Yukon College, opened in 1983, offers university transfer courses, trades training, professional and administrative studies and upgrading.

Economy and Industry

Economically the history of the Yukon has been one of "boom and bust." Since the discovery of major gold deposits in 1896, mining has been the backbone of the territorial economy. Total mineral production in 1995 was valued at $159 million. Gold accounted for almost 50% of that at $78 million. A new mining boom in the territory in 1996 doubled the number of people working in mining and exploration to approximately 2000.

Tourism: Currently tourism is the territory's second-largest private industry, employing about 3500 people. Almost 266 000 visitors contributed $60 million to the territorial coffers in 1995.

Government: The territory's economy is sustained principally by major financial grants from the federal government. Government continues to be the Yukon's main employer, providing jobs for 4500 people in 1995.

Employment: The total territorial workforce was 13 167 in 1994. Average unemployment was 9.5%. Average annual income in 1993 was $37 219.

Donjek River Valley, Kluane National Park

Social and Cultural Life

Museums: The Yukon has seven museums: the MacBride Museum, the Old Log Church Museum, and the Yukon Transportation Museum in Whitehorse; the Dawson City Museum in Dawson; the George Johnston Museum in Teslin; the Kluane Museum of Natural History in Burwash Landing; and the Keno Hill Mining Museum in Keno City.

Festivals: Major festivals are the Yukon Sourdough Rendezvous, the Frostbite Music Festival and the Yukon International Festival of Storytelling in Whitehorse; the Dawson City Discovery Days and Dawson Music Festival. The summer June Bug Music Festival in Haines Junction and the annual rodeo in Burwash are becoming increasingly popular.

Performing Arts: Amateur theatre and musical groups flourish all over the territory. In Whitehorse, the Frantic Follies, a professional group, have been entertaining summer visitors for a quarter of a century. The annual Rotary Music Festival in Whitehorse gives young musicians a chance to be coached by an expert outside adjudicator and to perform in public.

Sports and Recreation: Outdoor recreation is easily available most of the year. It ranges from fishing, canoeing, boating, hiking, mountain biking, horseback riding, camping and climbing in summer to cross-country skiing, skating, snowshoeing and snowmobiling in winter. Soccer, tennis, golf, softball, volleyball, squash and racquetball, along with hockey and curling, are all played enthusiastically in the Yukon. Orienteering is rapidly growing in popularity.

Historical Sites and Landmarks

Canol Road was built during the Second World War to link the oil wells at Norman Wells, Northwest Territories, to the refinery at Whitehorse. Remnants of the original pipeline, used for little more than a year, can still be seen along the road, as can abandoned Quonset huts and old wrecked trucks left behind after construction of the pipeline was completed.

Herschel Island, located just off the Yukon's short stretch of coastline on the Beaufort Sea, was a major whaling station in the late 1800s and a North West Mounted Police post from 1903 to 1940. Today it is a protected territorial historical park where evidence can still be seen of early occupations that include a 1000-year-old Thule and later Inuit settlements.

S.S. *Klondike* at Whitehorse was the largest sternwheeler to ply the Yukon River. Built in 1929, it sank in 1936 but was rebuilt the following year with the original machinery. It has since been restored and declared a National Historic Site.

Robert Service Cabin at Dawson City was for several years the home of the famous Bard of the Yukon who immortalized the Klondike Gold Rush in such classics as *The Cremation of Sam McGee* and *The Shooting of Dan McGrew*. The cabin has been declared a National Historic Site, and readings of Service's works are held there daily.

Jack London's Cabin and Interpretive Centre at Dawson City was briefly the home of American novelist Jack London, author of *White Fang* and *The Call of the Wild*. The centre features daily readings of London's works and an extensive photo exhibit.

Fort Selkirk was the site of the earliest trading post in the territory. The original post was destroyed and the site abandoned until the gold rush days when a North West Mounted Police post was built there. The later fort is still intact but accessible only by water.

Interesting Places to Visit

The Chilkoot Trail, long a symbol of the Klondike Stampede, is still a challenge. The 53-km (33-mi.) trail is rough, and weather can be extreme. It takes 3 to 5 days to complete, and hikers have to be in good condition and equipped for all weather. An average of 30 000 hikers use the trail annually.

Coal River Hot Springs is the territory's second territorial park and first ecological reserve. These glorious, remote hot springs are accessible only by helicopter from Watson Lake, 80 km (48 mi.) west. The springs are dramatic, a descending series of limestone terraces and pools of warm, bright-blue water, surrounded by lush vegetation. The whole reserve is virtually untouched.

Ivvavik (formerly Northern Yukon) *National Park* is dedicated to wilderness preservation and the maintenance of aboriginal lifestyles. Access to the park by fixed-wing aircraft requires prior permission. There are no visitor facilities and the entire 10 000 k^2 (3860 sq. mi.) area is wilderness. Whitewater rafting along the Firth River is the main recreational activity.

Takhini Hot Springs is a commercial development about a 20-minute drive north of Whitehorse. The pleasant pool has showers, changing rooms and a coffee shop. Also available are wooded campsites, barbecue pits, hiking and skiing trails, and a horse corral.

St. Barnabas – Bishop Bompas Memorial Church at Moosehide, now an abandoned village south of Dawson

Important Dates

Before 1741 As the glaciers that have covered most of North America recede, people spread out in the Yukon. They develop different languages and lifeways, gradually developing into several distinct First Nations. They live in the Yukon for thousands of years before Europeans "discover" the area.

1741 Vitus Bering, a Dane working for the Russian navy, sails from Siberia and sights the coast of North America.

1842 Hudson's Bay Company fur trader Robert Campbell builds the first fort in the Yukon, Fort Frances. HBC begins a fur trade with Yukon First Nations.

1867 Russia sells Alaska to the United States.

1891 Americans begin hunting whales off Herschel Island.

1895 A small detachment of North West Mounted Police bring Canadian law to the Yukon.

1896 Prospectors strike gold in the Klondike Valley near Dawson.

1897 News of the gold strike reaches the "outside." The Klondike Gold Rush begins.

1898 The gold rush is at its height. On June 13, the Yukon becomes a separate territory, divided from the North-West Territories.

1900 The White Pass and Yukon Railway is completed, running between Skagway, Alaska, and Whitehorse, Yukon.

1902 The federal government grants the Yukon a seat in the House of Commons.

1903 The Alaska boundary dispute is settled.

1907 Bank clerk and "Bard of the Yukon" Robert W. Service publishes his first book of "rhymes," *Songs of a Sourdough*.

1908 The Yukon has its first wholly elected council.

1911 A residential school for Native children is opened at Carcross.

1918 CPR steamer *Princess Sophia* sinks, drowning everyone aboard including many Yukoners.

1919 Silver and lead mining begins at Keno Hill.

1927 Airmail service to and from the Yukon begins.

1936 Martha Black becomes the second woman elected to the House of Commons.

1942 American troops and Canadian and American civilians begin construction of the Alaska Highway.

1953 The Yukon capital is moved from Dawson City to Whitehorse.

1964 Discovery of a huge lead-zinc deposit leads to the opening of Cyprus Anvil Mine at Faro

1969 A new town is built at Faro for the mine workers.

1973 Yukon's First Nations land claims negotiations begin.

1979 Governmental power is transferred from the Yukon's federally appointed commissioner and given to the elected representatives.

1983 The White Pass and Yukon Railway is shut down because of economic problems.

1985 The Yukon's first New Democratic Party (NDP) government is elected as a minority government, defeating the Progressive Conservatives. The Liberal Party elects two members to the legislature.

1987 NDP candidate Audrey McLaughlin is elected federal member of Parliament (MP) in a by-election.

1989 The New Democratic Party is re-elected with a majority.

1989 Audrey McLaughlin becomes national leader of the NDP, the first woman in Canada to lead a national party.

1991 An umbrella agreement is signed by the federal and territorial governments and the Council for Yukon Indians, establishing a basis for a land claims agreement.

1992 The NDP government is defeated. The Yukon Party, formerly the Yukon Progressive Conservative Party, forms a minority government led by John Ostashek.

1993 On May 29, 1993, the Council for Yukon Indians, the government of Canada and the government of the Yukon sign the Yukon Umbrella Final Agreement.

1994 Audrey McLaughlin resigns as official leader of the New Democratic Party.

1995 Centennial anniversary of the North West Mounted Police (now the Royal Canadian Mounted Police) in the Yukon.

1996 Centennial anniversary of the discovery of gold on Rabbit Creek, a tributary of the Klondike River.

1996 The Yukon party is defeated. The New Democratic Party forms a majority government led by Piers McDonald.

Important People

Laura Beatrice Berton (1878-1967), born in Ontario; teacher, writer; came to the Yukon to teach kindergarten in Dawson for "a year," married and stayed 25 years. Wrote *I Married the Yukon*, considered one of the finest books about the Yukon after the gold rush

Pierre Berton (1920-   ), born in Whitehorse and brought up in Dawson; writer, broadcaster; left the Yukon in 1932, but his books have introduced thousands to this remote territory; became Chancellor of Yukon College in 1988

George Black (1863-1965), born in New Brunswick; commissioner of the Yukon, 1912-1916, and Conservative member of Parliament, 1921-1936, when ill health forced him to resign; returned to politics in 1940 and was elected for two terms, serving one term as Speaker of the House of Commons

Martha Louise Black (1866-1957), born in the United States; crossed the Chilkoot Pass to join the Klondike Gold Rush; met and married George Black in 1904; during the First World War, accompanied Black and the Yukon Infantry Company to England, where she worked in the war effort; served as the Yukon's MP for one term, 1936-1940; awarded the Order of the British Empire in 1948; also known as an expert on Yukon wildflowers

Charlotte Selina Bompas (1830-1917), born in England; wife of Anglican Bishop Bompas, she worked alongside her husband in his missionary work in the Yukon and Northwest Territories; also lectured in England to raise money for the Yukon diocese

William C. Bompas (1834-1906), born in England; Anglican missionary, first Bishop of Athabaska, first Bishop of Mackenzie River and first Bishop of Selkirk (Yukon); returned to England only once during 43 years of church service in the Mackenzie and Yukon

Joseph Whiteside Boyle (1867-1923), born in Ontario, came to Dawson in 1897; entrepreneur, adventurer; made a fortune mining gold and became known as the "King of the Klondike"; outfitted and financed the Yukon Machine Gun Battery during the First World War; overseas during and after the war, acted as a trouble shooter and intelligence agent and was decorated by Britain, France, Russia and Roumania; dubbed the "Saviour of Roumania" for retrieving the Roumanian crown jewels and historical documents from Moscow after the Bolshevik Revolution and eventually

Pierre Berton

George Black

Martha Louise Black

Charlotte Bompas

negotiating a peace treaty between Russia and Roumania

Robert Campbell (1808-1894), born in Scotland; explorer, trader for the Hudson's Bay Company; first European to navigate and give English names to many rivers in southern Yukon; established a number of HBC posts, including Fort Frances and Fort Selkirk, which gave the company a monopoly over the fur trade

Ione Christensen (1933-   ), born in Dawson Creek, British Columbia, raised in Fort Selkirk, Yukon; mayor of Whitehorse and Yukon commissioner, Christensen was the first woman to hold both these positions

George Mercer Dawson (1849-1901), born in Nova Scotia; geologist, director of the Geological Survey of Canada, 1895-1901; in spite of physical handicaps resulting from a childhood illness, surveyed and mapped much of the Canadian Northwest and headed the first geological survey of the Yukon Territory; recognized as an authority on ethnology, archaeology and botany

Judy Gingell (1946-   ), born on her grandfather's trapline in southern Yukon; mixed Tuchone, Tagish and Tlingit Native ancestry; first Native Commissioner of the Yukon, appointed for a five-year term in June 1995; executive member of the Council for Yukon Indian Women's Association; President of the Yukon Indian Development Corp.; founding director of Northern Native Broadcasting

Hilda Hellaby (1917-1983), born in England; came to the Yukon in 1951; deaconess; worked for many years with immigrant Chinese people in Vancouver, where she was ordained in the Anglican Church; lived and worked all over the territory, mostly with Native people; awarded the Order of Canada in 1973; received the Commissioner's Award for her church and community work in 1983

Ted Harrison (1926-   ), born in England; came to the Yukon in 1968; his vivid, stylized paintings of the Yukon have won him admiration both inside and outside the territory; has also published several books illustrating his own stories and the poems of Robert Service

Chief Patsy Henderson (Kulsin) (1876-1966), born in Tagish of parents from the Alaskan coast; member of the Wolf Clan; was involved with the group that discovered major gold deposits in the Klondike; later in life, became chief of the Carcross people; as he grew older, spent many summer days at the railway station in Carcross, lecturing and telling visitors traditional stories of his people

Chief Isaac (1840-1932), born in the Dawson area; chief of the Moosehide band, which held by inheritance a large area of the interior Yukon, including the Klondike Valley; spoke out against the number of non-Natives trapping and hunting in his people's territory, pointing out that they interfered with the First Nations' traditional livelihood; affectionately known as Chief Isaac, Montezuma of the Klondike

Emma Joe (1883-1980), born in the Ross River district; leader of the Wolf Clan and a strong upholder of the traditions, qualities and virtues of her people; fostered and encouraged these in her family and the community; recognized as a great humanitarian leader

Margaret Joe (c. 1940-), born in Chilliwack, British Columbia; Native rights activist, politician; held many positions in Yukon First Nations organizations; elected to the Yukon Legislature in 1982, re-elected in 1985 and 1989; was the first Native woman in the Yukon to hold a cabinet position and held several from 1985 to 1991

Johnny Johns (1898-1988), born in Tagish; a noted Tagish singer, dancer, drummer, storyteller and poet; in 1942 was one of the main Native guides directing the American military engineers building the Alaska Highway; was also one of the top 10 big-game hunting guides in the world

Samuel T. Johnston (1935-), born in Teslin; politician; elder of the Teslin-Tlingit Band, first elected to the Yukon Legislature in 1985 as the New Democratic Party member for Campbell, re-elected in 1989; Speaker of the Assembly for both terms; started the Teslin-Tlingit Dancers in 1974 with family members; the dancers now have more than 20 members and perform traditional dances and songs throughout the Yukon and Alaska

William Judge (1850-1899); a Jesuit priest, known as the "Saint of Dawson City"; in 1898, built and operated Dawson's first hospital and church during the height of the Klondike Gold Rush; died of pneumonia after a brief illness, having literally worked himself to death

Jack London (1876-1916), born in California; writer; his novels and short stories, particularly *The Call of the Wild* (translated into 29 languages), were based on his experiences in the Yukon; stayed only a year, but his cabin in Dawson City is still a tourist attraction

Grant McConachie (1909-1965), born in Ontario; aviation pioneer; at the age of 22, McConachie was a bush pilot in

Chief Patsy Henderson

Margaret Joe

Johnny Johns

Samuel Johnston

119

William Judge

Audrey McLaughlin

John Ostashek

Robert Service

the Yukon and Northwest Territories; by the time he was 38, his small company, Yukon Southern Airlines, had become Canadian Pacific Airlines; his piloting exploits are documented in his book *Bush Pilot with a Briefcase*

Audrey McLaughlin (1936-), born in Ontario; came to the Yukon in 1979; first woman in Canada to lead a national political party — the New Democratic Party; also only the second woman in Yukon history to be elected MP for the territory

Jean-Marie Mouchet (1917-), born in France; missionary; came to Canada in the 1940s and to Old Crow in 1951; in 1955, set up a ski school for local children, called Territorial Experimental Ski Training (T.E.S.T.); one of his pupils, Martha Benjamin, was the first Yukoner to win a national ski title; the T.E.S.T. program extended to other communities and is still producing some of the territory's most talented athletes

Erik Hersholt Nielsen (1924-), born in Saskatchewan; politician; Conservative Member of Parliament for the Yukon from 1957 to 1987; strong defender of Native rights and Aboriginal title; held a number of ministerial posts and served as deputy prime minister from 1984 to 1987

John Ostashek (1936-), born in Alberta; guide, outfitter, politician; government leader of the Yukon Party, elected to Yukon Legislature from 1992-1996; at one time operated an air charter sightseeing business; was past president of the Yukon Outfitters Association

Robert W. Service (1874-1958), born in England; poet; came to Canada in 1896 and to the Yukon as a bank clerk in 1904; worked at the Bank of Commerce, first in Whitehorse, then in Dawson; resigned in 1909 to write full-time; left the Yukon in 1912; was a war correspondent in the Balkan war and an ambulance driver in the First World War

Angela Sidney (1902-1991), born near Carcross; the last of the Tagish people who still spoke the Tagish language and remembered the songs, dances and stories of the Tagish-Athapascans; published 4 books on these subjects; was awarded the Order of Canada in 1986

Elijah Smith (1912-1991), born in Hutshi Village, Yukon; Native rights activist, prominent Yukon elder and chief of the Kwanlin Dun Indian Band of Whitehorse; first president of the Yukon Native Brotherhood, forerunner of the Council for Yukon Indians; the driving force behind Canada's first Indian land claims paper, *Together Today for Our Children Tomorrow*

Samuel Benfield Steele (1849-1919), born in Ontario; commanded the NWMP post on the Chilkoot Pass in 1898, at the height of the Klondike Gold Rush; known for his kindness to those in need and for maintaining law, order and strict honesty; left the Yukon in 1899 to serve in the South African war; commanded the Second Canadian Contingent in the First World War

Isaac Stringer (1866-1934), born in England; Anglican missionary; known as "The Bishop Who Ate His Boots" for having done just that when he ran out of food on a dogsled trip between Fort McPherson (Northwest Territories) and Dawson City; spent most of his life doing missionary work in the North; fought against the inhumane treatment of Inuit by whaling captains at Herschel Island

Sarah Stringer (1869-1955), worked alongside her husband, Bishop Stringer, helping with his missionary work; lived on Herschel Island at the turn of the century, the first and only non-Native woman there for 8 years

Daniel Tlen (1949-), born in Burwash Landing; researcher, educator; has spent much of his adult life recording place names, myths and stories in First Nations languages; combined this with research at the Yukon Native Language Centre in Whitehorse; has developed and teaches an Athapaskan language curriculum

Emilie Tremblay (1870-1949), born in Quebec; came to the Yukon in 1894 to prospect with her husband, Pierre-Nolasque (Jack); in 1913 opened a dry goods and clothing store in Dawson and ordered dresses, hats and perfumes from Paris for the fashionable ladies of Dawson; the store, closed in 1940, is now an historical landmark

Hilda Pauline Watson (1922-1996), born in Saskatchewan; moved to Haines Junction in 1948; member of the first two-member executive committee that took the Territory's first steps toward responsible elected government; first elected leader of the Yukon government and first woman to lead a mainstream political party in Canada — the Yukon Territorial Progressive Conservatives, today the Yukon party

Florence Whyard (1917-), born in Ontario, has spent most of her life in the North; journalist, author, former Whitehorse mayor, Member of the Legislative Assembly and minister of Health; currently administrator for the Yukon, essentially assistant commissioner; is deeply involved in many service organizations, including the Red Cross and Imperial Order of Daughters of the Empire

Angela Sidney

Samuel Steele

Isaac Stringer

Daniel Tlen

Arctic Ocean
GREENLAND
Ellesmere Island
Beaufort Sea
Banks Island
Baffin Bay
ALASKA (UNITED STATES)
Inuvik
Dawson
Victoria Island
Baffin Island
Davis Strait
YUKON
Mackenzie
Great Bear Lake
Whitehorse
Arctic Circle
Iqaluit
NORTHWEST TERRITORIES
Baker Lake
Liard
Yellowknife
Great Slave Lake
Hudson Strait
Atlantic Ocean
Pacific Ocean
Slave
Ungava Bay
BRITISH COLUMBIA
Peace
Lake Athabasca
LABRADOR
Hudson Bay
Prince George
ALBERTA
MANITOBA
Labrador City
St. John's
Athabasca
SASKATCHEWAN
Churchill
Fraser
North Saskatchewan
Nelson
Edmonton
Flin Flon
James Bay
QUEBEC
NEWFOUNDLAND
Columbia
Vancouver
Lake Winnipeg
Gulf of St. Lawrence
PRINCE EDWARD ISLAND
Victoria
Calgary
Lake Mistassini
Sydney
Saskatoon
ONTARIO
NEW BRUNSWICK
Charlottetown
South Saskatchewan
Moncton
Regina
Quebec
Halifax
Thunder Bay
Winnipeg
Trois-Rivières
Fredericton
Montreal
NOVA SCOTIA
Sault Ste. Marie
Ottawa
Bay of Fundy
Red
Lake Superior
St. Lawrence
Ottawa
National Capital
Provincial Capital
Lake Huron
Toronto
Lake Ontario
Lake Michigan
UNITED STATES
Lake Erie
km
0 225 450 675 900 1 000
0 125 250 375 500 621.4
miles
100°
90°
80°

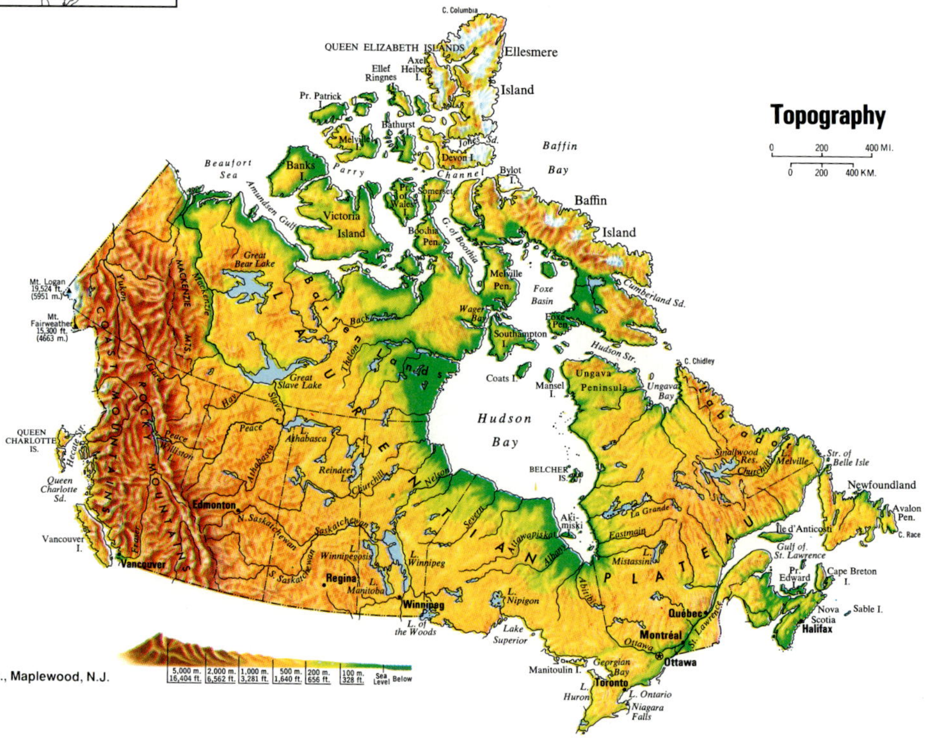

Topography
0 200 400 MI.
0 200 400 KM.
C. Columbia
QUEEN ELIZABETH ISLANDS
Ellesmere Island
Ellef Ringnes I.
Axel Heiberg I.
Pr. Patrick I.
Bathurst I.
Melville I.
Devon I.
Jones Sd.
Baffin Bay
Beaufort Sea
Banks
Parry Channel
Bylot I.
Baffin Island
Amundsen Gulf
Victoria Island
Pr. of Wales I.
Somerset I.
Boothia Pen.
G. of Boothia
Great Bear Lake
Melville Pen.
Foxe Basin
Cumberland Sd.
Mt. Logan 19,524 ft. (5951 m.)
Mt. Fairweather 15,300 ft. (4663 m.)
MACKENZIE MTS.
Yukon
Back
Thelon
Wager Bay
Southampton I.
Foxe Pen.
Hudson Str.
C. Chidley
Great Slave Lake
Coats I.
Mansel I.
Ungava Peninsula
Ungava Bay
Hay
Slave
Hudson Bay
QUEEN CHARLOTTE IS.
Peace
L. Athabasca
Queen Charlotte Sd.
Reindeer L.
Churchill
BELCHER IS.
Smallwood Res.
Churchill
L. Melville
Str. of Belle Isle
Newfoundland
Edmonton
N. Saskatchewan
Nelson
Akimiski I.
La Grande
Avalon Pen.
C. Race
Île d'Anticosti
Vancouver I.
Saskatchewan
L. Winnipegosis
Attawapiskat
Eastmain
Gulf of St. Lawrence
Vancouver
L. Winnipeg
Albany
Mistassini
Cape Breton I.
Pr. Edward I.
S. Saskatchewan
Regina
L. Manitoba
L. Nipigon
Nova Scotia
Sable I.
Winnipeg
Québec
Halifax
L. of the Woods
Lake Superior
Montréal
St. Lawrence
Ottawa
Ottawa
Manitoulin I.
Georgian Bay
Toronto
L. Huron
L. Ontario
Niagara Falls
LAURENTIAN PLATEAU
COAST MOUNTAINS
ROCKY MOUNTAINS
5,000 m. 16,404 ft.
2,000 m. 6,562 ft.
1,000 m. 3,281 ft.
500 m. 1,640 ft.
200 m. 656 ft.
100 m. 328 ft.
Sea Level
Below

YUKON TERRITORY
Recreation Area
Railway
Roads
Glacier
Spot Elevation
Capitals are underlined
City type size indicates relative importance
Metres
Feet
Above 4000
Above 13124
2000
6562
1000
3281
500
1640
200
656
0
0
200
656
Below 2000
Below 6562
0 50 100 150 200 km
0 50 100 mi
Scale 1:8 904 000
BEAUFORT SEA
Kaktovik
Herschel I.
Mackenzie Bay
BRITISH MOUNTAINS
IVVAVIK NATIONAL PARK
BRITISH MOUNTAINS
VUNTUT NATIONAL PARK
BROOKS RANGE
Arctic Village
Aklavik
Inuvik
Old Crow
Porcupine R.
Fort McPherson
Mackenzie R.
RICHARDSON MOUNTAINS
Fort Yukon
Yukon R.
Arctic Circle
Fort Good Hope
Great Bear Lake
Circle
UNITED STATES
CANADA
Fairbanks
ALASKA
Eagle
OGILVIE MOUNTAINS
Ogilvie R.
Peel R.
Big Delta
Tombstone Mtn 2192m
Castle Mountain 2365m
WERNECKE MOUNTAINS
MACKENZIE MOUNTAINS
NORTHWEST TERRITORIES
Boundary
Dawson
Bear Creek
Keno Hill
Mount Joy 2235m
BACKBONE RANGES
McQuesten
Mayo
KLONDIKE PLATEAU
Stewart Crossing
SELWYN MOUNTAINS
Keele Peak 2972m
Wrigley
Tanana R.
Northway
DAWSON RANGE
Yukon R.
Pelly Crossing
Beaver Creek
Snag
Minto
Faro
Ross R.
WRANGELL MOUNTAINS
Koidern
Carmacks
Big Salmon
Ross River
Tungsten
Mackenzie R.
PELLY MOUNTAINS
ST. CYR RANGE
BIG SALMON RANGE
Burwash Landing
Lower Laberge
LOGAN MOUNTAINS
Frances Lake
Nahanni Butte
Kluane
Canyon
KLUANE NATIONAL PARK
Mt. Logan 5959m
Mt. St. Elias 5489m
Haines Junction
Champagne
Whitehorse
Johnsons Crossing
Fort Liard
Watson Lake
Carcross
Tagish
Teslin
Rancheria
Morley River
Swift River
Upper Liard
Smith River
Gulf of Alaska
Skagway
CANADA
UNITED STATES
BRITISH COLUMBIA
Cassiar
148°
144°
140°
136°
132°
128°
124°
120°
68°
64°
60°

AVERAGE ANNUAL RAINFALL

Most of the Yukon receives less than 20 inches—500 mm—of rainfall each year.

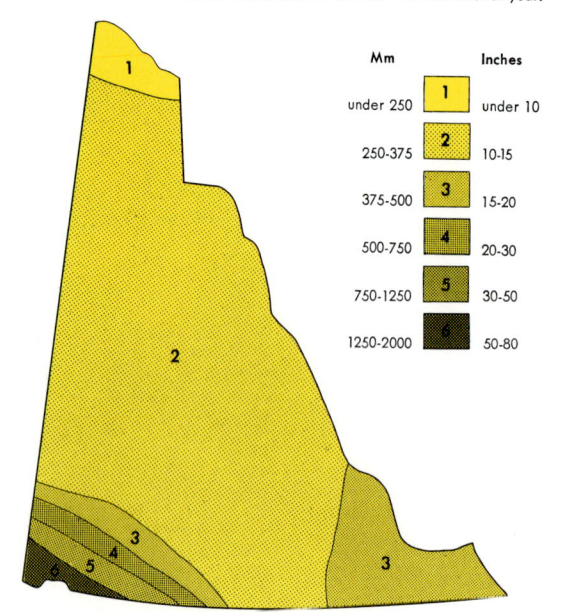

Mm		Inches
under 250	1	under 10
250-375	2	10-15
375-500	3	15-20
500-750	4	20-30
750-1250	5	30-50
1250-2000	6	50-80

Figures within areas are for identification purposes only.

GROWING SEASON

Most of the Yukon has a frost-free period of less than two months.

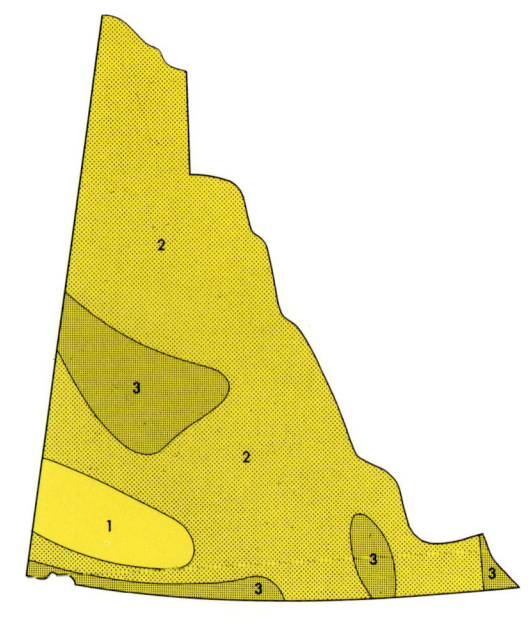

Average Number of Days in Frost-Free Period

| 1 | 0–40 | 2 | 40–60 | 3 | 60–80 |

Figures within areas are for identification purposes only.

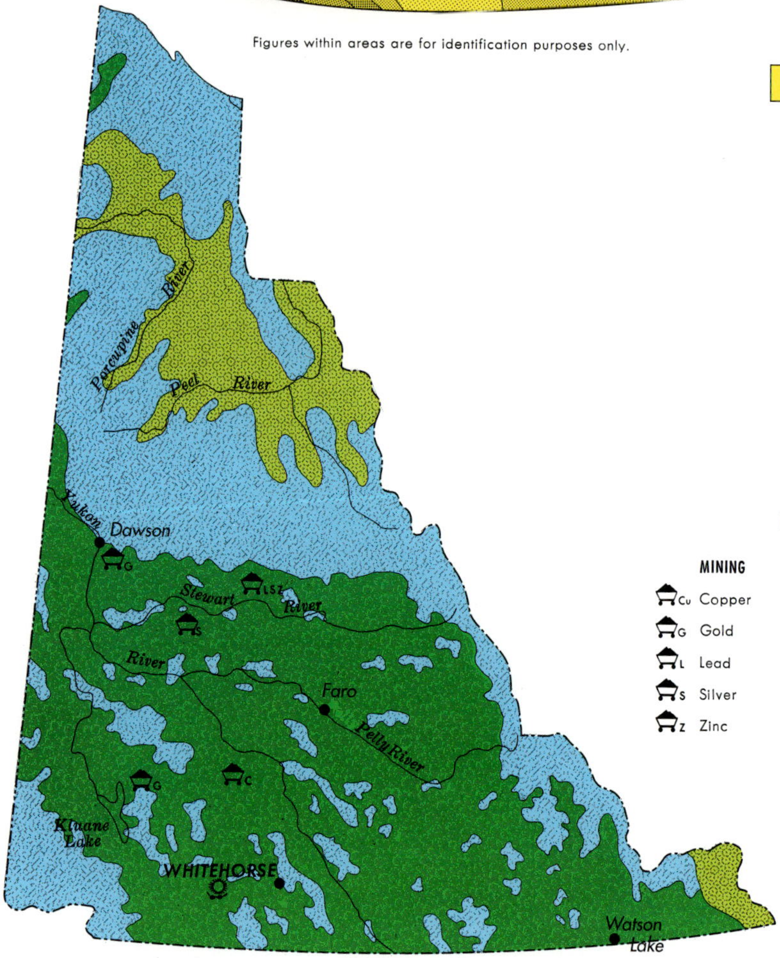

ECONOMY

MINING
- Cu Copper
- G Gold
- L Lead
- S Silver
- Z Zinc

OTHERS
- Tourists & Resorts

- Forests
- Alpine Forest—Tundra
- Barren or Ice-covered

Index

Page numbers that appear in boldface type indicate illustrations

air transport, 55-56, **56, 79, 107**
Alaska Boundary Dispute, 49
Alaska Highway, 7, 31, 57-60, **59, 72-73**
    communities along, 95-101
Alsek River, 14
animals, 19, 22-23, **22, 23,** 111
Arctic Circle, **19,** 106, **106**
Arctic Winter Games, **91,** 91-92
area, 9, 109
aurora borealis, 18, **18**
Beaver Creek, **100,** 101
Bell, John, 36
Bering Strait, 35
Bering, Vitus, 35
berries, 21, **21**
Berton, Laura Beatrice, 89, 117
Berton, Pierre, 89, 117, **117**
birds, 23, 111
    territorial bird, **108,** 109
Black, George, 55, 117, **117**
Black, Martha Louise, 89, 117, **117**
Bompas, Bishop William C., **37,** 39, **114,** 117, **118**
Bompas, Charlotte Selina, **37,** 117, **117**
borders, 9, 109
Boyle, Joseph Whiteside, 54-55, 117-18
Brooks Mountains, 9
Brooks Range, 9-10
Brown, Staff-Sgt. Charles, 40
Burwash Landing, **100,** 101
Campbell, Robert, 36, 118
Canol Road, 113
Carcross, 101, **102**
Carcross Desert, **11,** 101

caribou, 22-23, **22**
    hunting, 26-27, **27**
Carmack, George, 40, 41, **41**
Carmacks, 102
Chilkoot Pass, 38, 42, **43,** 44
Chilkoot Trail, 114
Christensen, Ione, 65, 118, **118**
climate, 15-17, 110
clothing, 87-88, **88**
Coal River Hot Springs, 114
Coast Mountains, 11
coat of arms, 109
commissioner, 63, 65, 111
communication, 78-79, 80
Constantine, Inspector Charles, 40
construction industry, 80
Council for Yukon Indians, 32
Court of Appeal, 70
Dawson City, **52,** 61, 63, 64, **66, 77, 95,** 103-104, **104**
    climate, 15, 16, 17
    festivals, 87
    gold rush, 42, 43, 44, 45-49, **46**
Dawson, George, 38, 103, 118, **118**
Dawson Nuggets, 90-91
daylight, 16
Dempster, Corporal W.J., 53
Dempster Highway, 105, **106**
    communities along, 105-107
Denali Fault, 10
Destruction Bay, 101
deWolfe, Percy, 48
dogsled racing, 92-93, **98**
Ecole Emilie Tremblay, 67-68, 112
education, 67-68, 111-12
employment, 76, 77, 78, 80, 112-13
Farley, Lilias, 88-89, **89**
farming, **81,** 82
Faro, 75, **76**
festivals, 85-86, **86,** 87, **87,** 113

fireweed (official flower), 20, **20, 108,** 109
first inhabitants, 25
First Nations, 25-33, **33,** 54, 83
    culture, 86, **87,** 87-88, **88, 89,** 97, **97,** 107, 118, 119, 120, 121
    education, 31, **31,** 37
    involvement in justice, 71
    land claims, 32-33
    language groups, **24,** 25-26
    lifeways, 26-29, **27, 28,** 30-32
    trade networks, **29,** 29-30
First World War, 54-55
Firth River, **107,** 114
fish, 23, 111
fishing, 82, **83**
Fitzgerald, Inspector Francis, 53, **53**
Five Finger Rapids, **16,** 102
flag, territorial, **108,** 109
flowers, **10,** 20-21, **20, 21,** 110-11
    territorial flower, **108,** 109
forest, 18-19, **19,** 110
forest fires, 19, 81
forestry, 80-81
Fort Frances, 36
Fort Selkirk, 36, 114
Fort Yukon, 36, **36**
Fortymile, 38, 43, **56**
Frantic Follies, 86, **86,** 113
fur trade, 35-36, 80
Gaslight Follies, **86,** 87
gem, territorial, 109
geography, 109-110
geology, 12-13
Gingell, Judy, 118
gold rush. See Klondike Gold Rush
government, 63-67
    as employer, 78, 112
    responsible government, 64-66
    territorial government today, 66-67, 111

Government of Canada, 39-40, 42, 49, 57, 63, 66, 67, 111
  Dept. of Indian Affairs and Northern Development, 65, 67
grizzly bears, **23,** 111
Haines Junction, **94,** 99-101
Harrison, Ted, 85, 88, **90,** 118, **118**
health services, 68-69
Hellaby, Hilda, 118
Henderson, Chief Patsy, 118, **119**
Henderson, Robert, 41
Herschel Island, 9, **110,** 113
historical sites and landmarks, 113-14
Holt, George, 38
Hudson's Bay Company, 35, 36, 80
hunting, 82-83
important dates, 115-16
important people, 117-21
interior mountains, 10
Inuit, 26
Isaac, Chief, 119
Ivvavik National Park, **107,** 110, 114
Jack London's Cabin and Interpretive Centre, 114
Joe, Emma, 119
Joe, Margaret, 119, **119**
Johns, Johnny, 119, **119**
Johnston, Samuel T., 119, **119**
Josie, Edith, 107
Judge, William, 119, **120**
justice, 69-71
Kaskawulsh Glacier, **11,** 101
Kathleen Lake, **71**
Keno City, **5**
Klondike Gold Rush, 7, 30, **34,** 40-49, **41, 43, 45, 46-47, 48,** 63
Klondike Highway, 79, **102**
  communities along, 101-104
Klondike River, 14, 40
Kluane Lake, **15**
Kluane National Park, **2-3, 9, 71,** 99, 101, **112**

Lake Laberge, 15
lakes, 15, **15, 17, 102,** 110
"Land of the Midnight Sun," **6,** 17
law and order, 39-40, 46-47
Law Courts Building, **70**
Legislative and Administrative Building, **62**
Legislature Chamber, **65**
Liard River, 14
literature, 89-90, 117, 119, 120
London, Jack, 89, 119
McConachie, Grant, 119-20
McDonald, Piers, 66
McGee, Sam, 90, **94**
Mackenzie Mountains, 9, 13
Mackenzie River, 14
McLaughlin, Audrey, 66, 120, **120**
maps of Canada
  political, **122**
  topographical, **122**
maps of Yukon
  average annual rainfall, **124**
  economy, **124**
  growing season, **124**
  physical, **123**
  roads, **96**
Midnight Dome, Dawson, 104
Miles Canyon, **13, 43, 77**
mining, 37-39, 40, 56-57, 74-76, **75, 76,** 112. *See also* Klondike Gold Rush
missionaries, 31, 37, 117, 120, 121
Moosehide, 114
Mouchet, Jean-Marie, 120
Mount Logan, 11, **12, 77,** 109
mountains, 9-11, **12,** 13, **13,** 35
Murray, Alexander Hunter, 36
museums, 98, 99, **100,** 103, **104,** 113
national parks, 110, 114
newspapers, 79
Nielson, Erik, 66, 120
North West Mounted Police, 40, 42-43, 44, 46-47, 48-49, **48, 53**

North-West Patrol Welcome Officer, **71**
northern lights, 18, **18**
Northern Yukon National Park. *See* Ivvavik National Park
Ogilvie Mountains, 10, **13**
Ogilvie, William, 44, 63
Old Crow, 106-107, **107**
Ostashek, John, 120, **120**
Peel River, 14, **14**
Pelly-Cassiar Mountains, 10
Pelly Crossing, **94,** 102
Pelly River, 14, **103**
performing arts, 85-87, 113
permafrost, 17, 58, **100**
Philipsen, Andrew A., 69
population, 9, 60-61, 109
Porcupine River, 14
Princess Sophia (ship), 55
prospectors, 37-39, 40. *See also* Klondike Gold Rush
public transit, 60
Rabbit Creek, 40, 41. *See also* Klondike River
radio, 78
railways, **50,** 51, **52,** 53, 79-80
recreation, 113
Richardson Mountains, 9, **10**
rivers, 13-14, **103, 107,** 110
roads. *See* Alaska Highway; Dempster Highway; Klondike Highway; Top of the World Highway
Robb, Jim, 89, **89**
Robert Service Cabin, **90,** 114
Roosevelt, President Theodore, 49
Ross, James H., 63
Royal Canadian Mounted Police, **39,** 40
Russia, 35
St. Elias Mountain, 35
Sam McGee Cabin, **94**
"Skookum Jim," 30, 40, **102**
Schwatka, Lt. Frederick, 38

126

Second World War, 57-59
Selwyn Mountains, 10, **10**
service industries, 80
Service, Robert W., 15, 89, **90**, 120, **120**
Sheardown, Sean, **91**, 92
ships, 51, 52, 55, 98, **98**, 113
Sidney, Angela, 120, **121**
Signpost Forest, 96, **97**
Silver City, **100**
Smarch, Keith Wolfe, 89, **89**
Smith, Elijah, 120
sports, 90-93, **91**, **92**, **93**, 113
S.S. Klondike, 98, **98**, 113
stagecoaches, 51-53
Steele, Supt. Samuel, 42, **48**, 120-21, **121**
Stringer, Bishop Isaac, **31**, 121, **121**
Stringer, Sarah, 121
surveyors, 38
"Tagish Charlie," 40, **46**, **102**
Tagish Lake, **4**
Takhini Hot Springs, 114
television, 79
terranes, 12-13
territorial council, 63-64, **64**

territorial parks, 110
territorial status, 63, 109
Teslin, 97, **97**
time zone, 110
Tintina Trench, 10
Tlen, Daniel, 121, **121**
Top of the World Highway, **104**, **105**
topography, 110
tourism, 77, **77**, 112
transfer payments, 74
transportation, 60, 79-80. *See also* air transport; Alaska Highway; Dempster Highway; Klondike Highway; railways; ships; stagecoaches
trees, 18-19, **19**, **109**, 110
Tremblay, Emilie, 121
trucking, 79, **79**
United States
  Alaska Boundary Dispute, 49
  building of Alaska Highway, 57-59
Victorian Order of Nurses (VON), 68, **69**
visual arts, 88-89, **89**
Walsh, Major James, 63

Watson, Hilda P., 121
Watson Lake, 61, 95-96, **97**
White Pass and Yukon Railway, **50**, 51, **52**, 53, 58, 79-80
Whitehorse, 69, 91, **91**, **94**, 97-99, **98**
  Alaska Highway construction, 58
  the city today, 60, 61, **61**
  climate, 15, 16, **16**, 17, 110
  festivals, 85-86
  territorial capital, 64, 109
Whyard, Florence, 121
wildlife sanctuaries, 110
Yukon Act, 63
Yukon College, 67, **68**, 112
Yukon Field Force, **48**, 68
Yukon International Storytelling Festival, 86, **87**
Yukon Machine Gun detachment, 54
Yukon Native Brotherhood, 32
Yukon Plateau, 10, 110
Yukon Quest, 92-93, **98**
Yukon River, **6**, 7, 13-14, **14**, **104**
Yukon Sourdough Rendezvous, 85-86, **86**

About the Author:

Anne Tempelman-Kluit is an award-winning author who has written countless articles about Yukon people and places. Born and educated in Britain, she has lived in Canada since 1961. Anne first visited the Yukon in 1964 and since then has lived and travelled all over the territory. She was a reporter for the *Whitehorse Star* and the Yukon columnist for *The Globe and Mail*. She spent three months rafting down the Yukon River, walked the length of the North Canol Road and covered the 1600-km (1000-mi.) Iditarod sled dog race across Alaska.

Picture acknowledgments

Abbreviations for location on page are, alone or in combination: T=Top, M=Middle, B=Bottom, L=Left, R=Right, I=Inset, BG=Background

Front cover, 10B, 11L, 14R, 16L, 20B, 61B, 75R, 76, 92L/R, 104TR, George Hunter/**Ivy Images;** 2-3, 86R, 87, 93 (both), 97BR, 99R, 100BL, 107B, 118B, 119MT/MB/B, 120MB, 121B, **Yukon Government;** 4, 14L, 16R, 19 (both), 21R, 88R, 94ML, 105, 108 (flower), back cover, **Paul von Baich;** 5, 6, 77T, 91BL, 97L, 98L, 102T, 104BL, 106L, 111, Richard Hartmier/**First Light;** 8, 12, 112, **Mike Beedell;** 10I, 22M, 33ML, 77BL, 79BL, 94MR, 110, 116, Patrick Morrow/**First Light;** 11R, 15, 18, 20TL, 21L, 22L/R, 23L/R, 59B, 61T (all), 68, 72-73, 79TL/R, 83TL/R, 86L/M, 88L, 91TL, 94T/BR, 98BR/TR, 99L, 100T/BR, 104TL, 108 (bird), W. Towriss/**Ivy Images;** 13R, 77BR, 108BG, 114, Steve McCutcheon/**Hot Shots;** 13L, Jason Puddifoot/**First Light;** 16M, 43TR/L, 45T, 52T, **Ivy Images;** 20TR, 21M, 75L, 97TR, 103, Steve Warble/**Ivy Images;** 24, 27 (both), **Gerald Lazare and Lewis Parker;** 28 (C2169), 29 (C2263), 34 (PA13443), 36, 43BR (C28676), 43BL (C15022), 45B (C5394), 46TL (C5393), 46BL (PA13444), 47 (C6648), 48R (PA16170), 53 (PA29622), 118MB (PA25520), 121MT (PA28146), **National Archives of Canada;** 31, 37 (both), 117B, 118T, 121MB, **Anglican Church of Canada, General Synod Archives;** 33TR, **Anne Tempelman-Kluit;** 33MR/MB/TL, 107T, **Tourism Yukon;** 33BR, George Petersen/**First Light**; 39, **The Conferation Life Gallery of Canadian History;** 41, **Provincial Archives of Alberta/H. Pollard Collection;** 46BR, 52B (Scharschmidt Collection), 54, 59T, 64, 119T, 120T (MacBride Museum Collection), 56 (Claude Tidd Collection), 90R (Gillis Collection), 117MT/MB (Betts Collection), 118MT (Yukon Executive Council Collection), 121T, **Yukon Archives;** 48L, 53I, **Royal Canadian Mounted Police Archives;** 50, 81 (all), 94BL, 102B, **Gary Fiegehen;** 62, 71I, 85BL, Ken Straiton/**First Light;** 65, 66, 70, 71, A.E. Sirulnikoff/**First Light;** 69R, **Provincial Archives of B.C.;** 69L, **Metro Toronto Library Board;** 84, **Courtesy of Ted Harrison;** 89L, **By permission of Jim Robb and the Yukon Permanent Art Collection, managed by the Friends of the Gallery;** 89M, **By permission of Keith Wolfe Smarch, Collection of Marg and Rolf Hougan;** 89R, **By permission of Catherine Regehr and the Yukon Permanent Art Collection, managed by the Friends of the Gallery;** 90L, **By permission of Kids Can Press, illustration © 1986 by Ted Harrison;** 91R, **Canada Games Council;** 104BR, Winston Fraser/**Ivy Images;** 106R, Stephen Krasemann/**Hot Shots;** 117T, CBC/**Fred Phipps Photo;** 120MT, **Courtesy of New Democratic Party;** 120B, **McClelland & Stewart.**